ATLANTIC CROSSING

Barbara Molin

ISBN-9798649954044

Printed by KDP

For my sons, Justin and Ryan.

Author's Notes

- Throughout the book, I used feet for depth and height because in 2004, I was using second-hand charts and the depths were still marked in feet and fathoms. When we reached Portugal I had access to new charts and cruising guides and so the depths are in meters.
- I used Canadian English spelling throughout the book except when James is speaking in the Yorkshire dialect.
- I decided not to include a glossary of sailing terms or a diagram of sailboat with parts labelled. I am assuming that a reader who will pick up this book will have read a few sailing books before mine and already have a knowledge of sailing terms.

If you look for perfection, you'll never be content.
Leo Tolstoy

1. The beginning

Paradise is not a place, it's a state of mind.

May 2004.

Mozart's Concerto No. 5, pours out of the speaker in the cockpit. Drops of sweat run down my neck and chest into the crevice between my breasts and over my stomach, as I dip a brush into a can of varnish. I carefully spread the golden liquid on the teak trim of my new sailboat, its turpentine smell overpowering the scent of the sea. I am lost in the moment as I try to match brush strokes to the rhythm of the music.

But it is too hot to varnish any longer. I sigh as I return the brush into an old jar, half full of mineral spirits and then pound the lid of the can closed tight with a hammer. Splatters of varnish cover my legs, hands and bikini. I wet a piece of paper towel in the brush cleaner and wipe off the biggest ones before screwing back the top of the jar. While stretching muscles stiff from sitting on the teak deck all morning, I glance around at the boat. Like make-up on a pretty woman, the shiny surface of the varnish has transformed her into a beautiful yacht. A satisfied grin pushes its way onto my face.

I stand up, raise my arms, take a deep breath and stretch, letting my eyes relax into the distance. Approximately forty boats are left in Elizabeth Harbour anchorage, down from four hundred at Christmas. Soon everyone will be gone. I take off my raffia hat, grab a mask and snorkel off the cabin top, and jump into the sea.

The water is only slightly cooler than the air, but I love the feel of the salty liquid, as I stroke through its surface around the boat. Checking the hull, keel and rudder for barnacles, I note that the bottom paint is still working at keeping them off.

I swim to the bow and look up. The word, 'Eidos' is stencilled in large letters on both sides against a navy blue background of the trim. I searched on-line and finally found the meaning in a Scrabble dictionary. Essence in Greek. There was also a Greek goddess called Aidos but she was a goddess of shame, modesty, respect and humility and that doesn't fit. Eidos is not ashamed, modest or humble. She loves to shine. I prefer essence. She is my home, my magic carpet and contains everything I need. According to her designer, she is capable of taking me anywhere in the world, having the right balance of beauty, strength, comfort and speed. Big enough for two, yet small enough so that I can handle her on my own.

A dolphin mother and her baby frolic in the distance. They sometimes swim nearer but she is protective and won't let anyone close. With my face in the water, I follow the snaking anchor chain, lying on the bottom. My eyes straining, I see the CQR anchor ten feet down, dug deeply into the sand among the coral heads, holding firmly. I swim back and climb up the ladder that hangs off the stern. I rinse off with a bucket of fresh water and squeeze the remaining drips out of the ends of my hair.

A man and a woman approach in their rubber dinghy from a ketch anchored nearby. They wave and I wave back. The man puts the outboard into neutral, and the dinghy coasts toward Eidos.

"Beautiful day, isn't it?" the woman says.

"Yup. It has all the ingredients to make it

perfect. Sun, sea, blue sky, and sand," I reply.

"Are you alone?"

"Yes."

"Oh, so you're a single-hander. That's impressive."

"I had a crew from Florida, don't really like sailing alone."

She nods. "My name is Eileen Quinn and I'm a musician, and this is my husband, David. Our boat is called Little Gidding," she says, pointing to the ketch.

"Hi, I'm Barbara."

"How long are you staying in the Bahamas?" David asks.

"Another month. How about you?"

"We're heading south next week. Venezuela for the hurricane season. Where will you go?"

"Not sure yet. I need to find a crew."

"Well, perhaps you'll find someone tonight. I'm organizing a musical evening and a potluck dinner on the beach. The last one of the season. Will you come?"

"Of course, thank you."

They slowly motor away toward another boat and I go inside to make lunch.

In the afternoon I sit in the cockpit under the

shade of the canvas awning and weave palm fronds into a basket, while the sun descends through the fluffy clouds astern. I stop only when my fingers, unused to the movements begin to ache. In three long days, I've made three small baskets and two coasters. I find it hard to believe how these objects can be so inexpensive back in Canada considering the labour involved.

The sound of conch horns echoes through the anchorage. I lift my head from my work and watch as the sky turns crimson and then, in a blink of an eye, black. Other horns follow. It's a sunset ritual here and usually, at least one person pays attention. My neighbours' daughter, who can't be older than six blows the best, so it's not a function of lung power. I'd like to make one, but there are only so many hours in the day, and right now my newest obsession is basket weaving. Joy and Bea have been teaching anyone interested and almost every woman here is making them.

I gather up my weaving and step down into the cabin, turn on the light above the galley, and reach past the chart table to flip the switch for the anchor light.

The minor chords of guitar strumming waft in from the beach, so I quickly make a salad and fill a picnic basket. I wrap a pareo around my waist, grab a scarf for my shoulders and climb down into the dinghy.

A bonfire on the beach shows me the way. Dozens of dinghies are already parked on the sand, others motoring behind me. I step into the shallow water and pull the dinghy on to the shore.

Eileen is tuning her guitar while David adjusts the speakers. A small generator hums behind a tree. The picnic tables are laden with food, bottles of wine, plates, and glasses. Candles in jars light the feast. People move in and out of shadows. Children and teens mingle with adults. A woman is nursing a baby in a hammock strung between two palm trees. Conversation and laughter surround me. A group of women wrapped in muumuus and pareos are playing Mexican train at another table, an oil lamp illuminating the dominoes. Few people sit on stools around a counter at the nearby beach bar.

Several men surround the smoking drum-half barbecue. They have been spearfishing the reefs today and the grill is full of fish, their distinctive scent permeating the air. I nod to one of them, Paul, who is wearing a t-shirt picturing a skeleton sitting on a bench. "Waiting for the perfect woman," it says. He had invited me over to see his new motor yacht a few days ago.

"Oh, by the way, I prefer short hair on women, I hate finding lose hair on the floor of the shower. Would you consider cutting yours?" he had asked me after the tour of his boat.

"Sorry." I said, wishing I dared to add, 'I hate powerboats'. I'd like to find a man with whom to share this lifestyle, but Paul and I certainly don't have the same values.

Many of the cruisers come to Elizabeth Harbour every winter and know each other well. I've been here for the past five months, and recognize a few familiar faces. Sue waves me over. John opens a bottle of wine and fills our glasses. I put the salad on the table. I tell them what Paul said. Both Sue and John have long ponytails. Their boat, Two Dreams, is their winter home. In summer, they ride Harleys. That's their other dream. Sue pulls a hairbrush out of her bag, stands up, and pulls off the elastic band from her hair. She nods to me to do the same. And then we both brush our hair, tipping our heads upside down and flicking them up, like horses' manes, laughing. I sneak a look toward the barbeque to see if Paul is watching but can't see in the dark.

"You know," I say to Sue and John, "considering how transient this community of boaters is, I feel that I have finally found my tribe.

I'll miss it. I'll miss you."

"I know what you mean," says Sue.

"Where are you going for the hurricane season?" I ask them, as John tops up our glasses.

"Back to Florida. We'll haul out Two Dreams and then go riding west. Possibly as far as California. Will you be sailing to Canada?"

"No. I am done with Canada. Too far, too cold, and too many bad memories. I need a new life. I want to sail to Europe."

"That's ambitious."

"A man once gave me this advice, love where you live, love what you do, love who you're with. I know I've got the first two covered."

Greece beckons. Always has. A country of ancient ruins, history, deep roots, where old people are respected. The last time I was there on a holiday, I met a couple on a sailboat just completing their circumnavigation. I decided then and there that cruising would be the best way to explore its hundreds of islands. But to cross the Atlantic, alone? Many people have done it. They've written books about it. Perhaps I could too. I've done one overnight passage along the coast of Florida after buying Eidos, and several longer ones as crew. At least on the open ocean, there are no rocks to hit. But I am terrified of facing storms alone, getting hurt with no one to help. And loneliness. That's the worst.

We speak of our plans for the summer but that's as far ahead as we're willing to commit. We mingle with the others on the beach, chat, say goodbyes, exchange email addresses, smile for photographs. I buy a CD from Eileen and thank her and David for the invitation. David mentions that he also is a writer, and wants to interview me for an article on single sailors. We promise to keep in touch.

The music grows louder and Eileen sings her final song. The rest of us gather around and join in on the chorus.

I've got seashells,
I've got souvenirs
I've got songs I've penned
I've got photographs
I've got memories
But mostly, I've got friends.

Tears fill my eyes and roll down my face but I don't care. It doesn't matter yet it does, that in a month I'll probably never see any of these people again, knowing that the sense of community travels with the wind and the tide and can be found wherever boaters gather.

I say goodbye to Sue and John, gather up my things and in the dark, alone and miserable stumble to the dinghy.

2. Searching for crew

Better the devil you know than the devil you don't.

The next morning, coffee next to me on the table, I sit in the cockpit, open the laptop and edit my latest article for a sailing magazine. There is no rush or due date, but the sooner I submit it, the sooner there is a chance an editor will buy it and I'll get some money deposited into my bank in Canada. I'm running short again.

I find it difficult to concentrate. My mind wanders to last night's conversation with Sue and John.

Elizabeth Harbour is called Chicken Harbour by cruisers for a reason. It's relatively close to Florida, safe, and the locals are friendly. There are shops, services, and Internet access at the telephone office in George Town, a short dinghy ride away. There is even a small airport nearby.

Many cruisers gather here to wait for a weather window and prepare for the next passage, usually to Turks and Caicos, the next country south in the Caribbean. But the Bahamian islands south of Elizabeth Harbour – Long Island forty miles away, Crooked Island a hundred miles further, and Mayaguana another sixty are sparsely populated with no one to call for help if one gets into trouble. To sail to the Turks and Caicos directly, about 275 miles away, would take three days and nights if the wind was favourable. And if the wind came from the east, as it usually does in this area, the passage would involve a hard slog to windward, adding who knows how much time. And so, many cruisers stop here and never go any further, chickening out in Chicken Harbour all winter and head back home to the U.S. for the duration of the hurricane season.

Heading north for me is out of the question. I would have to pay sales tax on Eidos in Florida and I simply don't have the money. Tax is due three months after sale date and I've already used that up. And then, of course, there is the hurricane season. Most of this area is at risk of a hit even as far as Georgia and Texas. People with money haul out their boat on land or tuck it away in a marina and pray for the best.

To sail south to Venezuela, and out of the danger zone would mean a series of overnight jaunts for the next month. Alone. Other cruisers have reported pirate attacks near Venezuela. Scary.

West to Panama, weaving among the Caribbean islands feels even more intimidating. All of these routes involve crossing the hurricane zone.

And then, there is the open Atlantic. If I sail to Bermuda, and then to the Azores, Eidos should be safe. But it's a long way to sail. Each path is fraught with danger.

I need help.

I close the laptop, put a dress on, throw my sandals into the dinghy and go to town. I tie up at the dinghy dock, and walk along a dusty road, past colourfully painted cottages. Local women stare at me from the doorways, their chocolate skin gleaming in the sunlight. At the telephone office, I email the new article, check messages, and post some ads on-line seeking crew. There is an email from Ryan, my older son living in Taiwan, thanking me for attending his wedding. He went there to teach English and met another teacher, a local girl. Justin, the younger one, sends some photos he took while visiting me in January. My sister, Isha is asking about my plans and whether our parents know where I am. I make a note to call them soon.

During the next few days, I receive responses from people who are interested in crewing but want to be paid. There are two weeks left before my tourist visa runs out. I try not to think about it, but I know I will have a panic attack any day.

One evening, as I check the boat before going to bed, I look around the anchorage. The stars shower the inky sky. My hair blows in the breeze as I watch the clouds scoot across the sky obliterating the moon. I squint my eyes to imagine what it would be like if the sails were up, no shore lights, no anchor lights. Pitch black, just me and the sea, the sky, and the stars. Could I do it?

The next day, as an afterthought, I email my ex-boyfriend. James is nine years younger and has been travelling most of his life after falling out with his father who wanted him to take over the family business. We had met in Mexico four years ago. He had just bought a small sailboat "for a dollar," and had taught himself to sail by crossing the 300 nautical miles between Puerto Vallarta and La Paz.

"For the first few days, I just drifted around. Had no idea what to do. Finally, I figured out what string to pull," he had told me.

I was in La Paz having just left another boat, that I had crewed on and had also bought a small sailboat to live on. On our first date, we sat on the edge of a sidewalk, next to a shack selling snacks, and shared a can of beer.

"What do you want in life?" he had asked me.

"I want to sail around the world but not alone," I said.

"In that case, I am your man."

Soon we were spending more and more time together on board "Fenix," my 27-foot Folkboat, while he was selling gear from his at monthly boat jumbles. Eventually, he sold the nearly empty boat as well and moved onto mine. For the next two years, we sailed together up and down the Sea of Cortes in winter and travelled to the US and Europe in summer. But Fenix was too small for two people to live on board full time and cross oceans. We couldn't even stand up inside her small cabin. And so, we spent several months looking for a bigger boat, for our planned circumnavigation. But as time went on, I realized that James didn't want to make our relationship permanent, didn't want to share the ownership of the new boat, only wanted to come as my crew. He still needed his freedom. And his beer as I had realized much too late. And so, eventually, we went our separate ways.

He replies the next day and asks about Eidos.

"She's 32-feet, a cutter-rigged sloop, fibreglass, 1980," I tell him. "Ted Brewer design, a strong pocket cruiser." I email him a copy of the survey.

We talk on Skype. He is in Yorkshire visiting his family.

"What route? Straight across?"

"No, Bermuda, Azores and Portugal."

"Oh, good, I know a woman in Bermuda. How long will it take?"

"About six weeks, give or take."

"How soon?" he asks.

"Two weeks. My cruising permit expires June third."

"I'll look into flights, maybe visit a friend in Toronto on the way down, but I can only stay for six weeks, eight max. And you pay for food."

A huge weight lifts off my shoulders. Before we met, James crossed the Australia desert alone with his Landrover. He's hunted with the Inuits in Alaska. He travelled to Columbia when it was on the do-not-travel list. He survived a tsunami in the Philippines. He is used to sleeping in fleabag hotels, bus shelters, airports and even the occasional ditch at the side of the road. He makes friends easily and is often invited to visit. When we travelled together through the U.S., we delivered cars from one city to another, so we had free transport. He finances his lifestyle by buying something cheaply and selling it for profit or by getting a job driving.

'I can drive anything, a combine or a tour bus,' he had told me.

He can be rude, rough and abusive especially when he is drinking, but he is smart, tough and good at solving problems. If anything happens to me, he will get us across.

I spend the next two weeks preparing. I stock up on food in George Town and email another article to Sail magazine. Finally, I refill the propane tank for the galley stove, top up with water, diesel for the engine, and gas for the dinghy, ferrying five-gallon containers from George Town and using block and tackle to raise them onto the deck.

June 1st, the day James is to arrive, I take a taxi to the airport and wait behind a chain-link fence separating the parking lot from the airport. He looks fit and healthy even with his pale pink, untanned, English skin, and sporting the usual buzz cut because, 'If I get into a fight, the other guy can't grab it.' He's carrying a huge backpack and wearing heavy hiking boots ('for protection from mad dogs'), the one extravagance he allows himself for the adventurous life he leads.

"You're looking old," he greets me. "You've got more wrinkles than the last time I saw you. Is the boat ready?"

3. Good bye Bahamas

Oh, King Poseidon
We call upon you, the God of the Ocean
Please protect us
Because we are small and the ocean big
and we are afraid.
Amen.

Thursday, June 3.

At noon, we are standing at the stern of the boat, glasses in hand.

"To a safe voyage," I tip a toast of brandy into the calm, azure water for luck and then take a sip, savouring the smooth taste of the amber-coloured liquid.

"You're wasting it," says James, as he empties

his glass in one gulp. "Let's get moving."

"We've got to do it to stay safe. It's a tradition. Just like not leaving on a Friday." I squint my eyes at him and put the glasses and bottle away.

There is a light, cool southeast breeze blowing into the bay, taking the sting from the sun's heat. James makes his way to the bow, then pulls up the anchor chain hand over hand letting it fall into the locker. I turn the engine on to idle and grab the steering wheel.

"You really should have a better set-up to secure this anchor," he turns his head to me, as the shank of the 25-pound CQR clunks on the bow-roller. "That pin doesn't look strong enough. Have you got a shackle?"

"Not sure. I'll look later."

Free of her grip on the sea bottom, Eidos begins to drift. I put the engine in forward and we weave our way through one of the largest natural harbours in the world. The last of the anchor-outs, my friends and neighbours for the past six months wave to us goodbye from the cockpits of their boats as we pass. I steer with one hand and wave with the other, my eyes flicking between the boats and the depth sounder display mounted on the cabin bulkhead with the wind speed indicator next to it.

"Watch out for the coral heads," I call to

James. Eight feet. Seven. Eight. Ten. With the sun overhead, we can easily see their jagged teeth among the white sand, seemingly only inches beneath the surface of the clear water.

James scans the sea ahead and films the pale, palm tree and shrub-covered islands and cays. We are nearing the cut that separates the anchorage from the open sea.

"You're in the clear, deep water ahead," he says.

"As long as we're heading into the wind, you might as well put the main up," I call out while taking the main sheet off the cleat

He puts the camera in the pocket of his shorts and walks toward the mast.

"So, how old is your rigging?" he asks, as he releases the ties holding the sail on the boom and hoists it up with the halyard. His eyes follow the rising sail and scan the top of the mast.

"Not sure, but you've seen the survey and I've tested it between Florida and here."

Once we clear the last of the barrier reefs, I unfurl the jib and cleat off its sheet on the port side. James secures the main sheet and takes the helm, while I turn off the engine. Eidos surges forward like a filly let out of a paddock.

Now there is only the sound of the wind

filling the sails and the swish of the hull through the Atlantic swell. I close my eyes and take a deep breath. The scent of the sea fills my nostrils. My hair flies away from my face, teasing the side of my neck. I pull an elastic band from my pocket and tie it back into a ponytail.

I step under the blue canvas spray-hood into the main cabin and turn on the VHF radio above the chart table. We need to check out before leaving.

"Elizabeth Harbour Authority, Elizabeth Harbour Authority, this is the sailing yacht, Eidos."

"Eidos, this is Elizabeth Harbour Authority."

"Elizabeth Harbour Authority, we are leaving the Bahamas, thank you for your hospitality."

"Where are you headed, Eidos?"

"Bermuda."

"Have a safe voyage, Eidos."

"Thank you."

Picking up a pencil, I draw a small circle with a cross through it, to mark our position on the chart and check the GPS for our distance to sail.

"It's 788 nautical miles at 50 degrees to Bermuda," I call out to James.

"Hell of a long way."

"Eight or nine days on the same tack, if the wind holds."

We are enjoying a steady trade wind from the starboard beam. This morning's weather forecast promised more fair weather for the next few days.

I climb back to the cockpit to look around for any ships in the area. James is sitting next to the wheel, water bottle topped with a funnel between his legs. A sheet of paper towelling is inside the funnel. He is pouring water into the funnel from a gallon jug, one of the extra ones I have to extend the water supply for the trip.

"This water is shite," he says." It's got crap in it."

"I've been drinking it all along. It's just silt on the bottom."

"It doesn't look like silt, it looks like shite. You should have cleaned out the tanks."

"I have, and I put bleach in them in Florida."

"It smells like bleach all right. How much did you put in?" He says, taking a sniff.

"Just a cap full."

"You put in too much. Now we have to filter it before drinking."

I take a deep breath and go below again. There is no point in continuing this conversation, or I'll end up defending my whole life soon. Drinking water in the Bahamas is what it is, sometimes better, other times worse and since it hasn't rained since the previous summer, it was nearing the end of the supply. You either drink what there is, or pay sixty cents a gallon for desalinated water. Paying thirty-six dollars to fill the tanks for something I could get for free at the dinghy dock was not in my budget.

In the afternoon we get hit by a small squall, but it's not dangerous, it briefly provides us with shade and cools the air.

I make vegetable soup for early dinner, over the gimballed, propane stove in the small galley on the port side of the boat. From here, I can see behind the boat through the open hatch and if needed, reach the VHF radio almost without moving. To my left is the deep, insulated icebox, where I store fresh food. We don't have ice in it-- it would melt in an hour. Aft of the icebox, a shelf holds plates, mugs and bowls. In front of me, the three-burner stove with an oven hangs on a couple of massive bolts. It keeps level no matter what the waves are doing. Behind it, there are cupboards for canned goods, pasta, flour and rice and above a porthole to take away some of the heat from the cooking. To my right is a counter with two covered deep bins. One has all the pots and pans in it and the other bottles of oil, vinegar, and wine. And finally a small sink. Above the counter are three cupboards holding coffee, tea, sugar, spices, raisins, nuts and other small items. Under the sink are two drawers for cutlery and large utensils. Everything close by and convenient.

We eat the soup with a slice of bread in the cockpit, in silence, looking around at the disappearing land behind us absorbing the enormity of our situation.

"It's a long way to go," says James. "Are you sure you want to do it? We can still turn back."

"Can't turn back now. My visa has expired and they will not renew it. But I feel excited. Don't you?"

"We've never done anything like this. We might not make it."

"It's a strong boat and I don't think we'll kill each other."

After the meal, James lowers a bucket on a string into the sea, fills it with the clear water and washes the dishes while I dry and put them away.

We'll both be sleeping, one at a time in the quarter berth on the starboard side, aft of the chart table and partly under the cockpit seat where the boat's motion is the gentlest. We'll be hot-bunking, so that when the person coming off watch is cold and tired, the bunk will be warm from the other person having just left it. I had stowed all unneeded gear in the forward cabin, its door firmly closed. The toilet is up forward as well, on the port side. James' backpack lies on the port settee behind the dining table. Rain jackets, life jackets and safety tethers are ready if needed on the starboard settee. There are shelves for books above the settees.

"You should be out here for the sunset before you go to bed," James calls out.

I climb up the ladder into the cockpit, as the flaming orange globe kisses what remains visible of the low-lying islands behind us on the darkening horizon. The sky lights up as if on fire with smoky, cotton ball clouds among the flames and then darkness surrounds us. I look toward the east, and on the other side of the horizon, the full moon is just emerging from the sea. It floods the ocean's surface with its beam, like a spotlight lighting our way over the black sea. There are a few clouds in the sky, but the moon sheds them as if sliding out from under a white, fluffy, down duvet.

"This is nice," says James.

"Sure is."

I switch on our navigation lights. Behind, an inter-island freighter crosses our wake, and I feel a little sad to be leaving the Bahamas, already missing its friendly people, the safety of the anchorage and the warm weather. It is not likely that I will be back soon.

Finally, I am too tired to keep my eyes open any longer, take a final look around and return below, and in the semi-darkness crawl into the quarter berth. James has the first watch.

The sharp clang of the aluminium boom and raucous rattle of a winch spinning jerks me from sleep, heart pounding. I scramble out of the bunk cave and stagger to the cockpit.

"What's going on?"

"Had to tack," James yells over the noise of the sails snapping, as he cranks on the winch handle. "Current's pushing us too close to that island."

I help him with the jib by tailing the end of the sheet. Once we're done, heart still beating wildly, I return below, flick the red chart table light on and check the cabin clock: 22:05.

"What's our position?" James has a better view of the GPS.

"24 03 point 3 north. 75 29 point 8 west."

I measure off the numbers on the edge of the chart and mark our position. Then I spread the dividers, one leg on the dark blue of the shallows, the other on the centre of the cross and read off the distance on the latitude scale.

"Three miles south of the reefs at Devil's Point on Cat Island," I call back to him. What have you been steering?"

"30 degrees magnetic."

I put on a sweatshirt and return to the cockpit.

"This boat doesn't sail worth a damn," James says. "The best she'll do is 120 from one side to the other. I've got the sails trimmed as much as I can and we're now going south, back where we came from."

We raced my previous boat, Fenix in La Paz and even won once, so I trust his skills. It's Eidos that's at fault here, a boat made for comfort, not racing. Her sails are old and baggy, and difficult to trim.

"I don't want to be here all night with this light breeze and we still have Columbus Point to clear ahead. Let's get out of here. Engine?" I ask, longing to be back in my bunk.

"Engine."

I turn the key, relieved as the 20 horse-powered Yanmar rumbles to life. James points Eidos' bow back on course while I roll up the jib.

By three o'clock in the morning, we are safely past Devil's Point, clear of Columbus Point, and out in the open ocean once again under sail.

4. Out of sight of land.

Why upon your first voyage as a passenger, did you yourself feel such a mystical vibration,
when first told that you and your ship were now out of sight of land?
Why did the old Persians hold the sea holy?
Why did the Greeks give it a separate deity, and make him the own brother of Jove?
Surely all this is not without meaning.
-Herman Melville, Moby Dick

Friday, June 4.

I wake up, crawl out of the bunk and take a look outside, yawning. The sun is sliding from under the sea like a yellow beach ball popping out of water. The sails are pulling us toward it. I am blinded looking forward. There are no ships anywhere.

"Nice day. How was the rest of the night?" I ask James, who is slathering sunblock on his face and neck.

"A few ships in the distance but not bad."

"Shall we have the usual for breakfast?"

"Might as well. As long as you can cook, I can eat."

I put the water on for coffee and then pass him two potatoes, an onion, garlic, the chopping board, and a knife. He cuts, and I stir the vegetables and the beans in a pan over the flame, adding three eggs at the end. I pass the plates and forks and bring with me the bread and the coffee mugs.

"I've rigged a bungee cord from the wheel to the cleat to keep the wheel steady," he shows me. "Now we don't have to hold on to the wheel all the time and the boat stays on course. More or less."

Eidos has a long fin keel with a skeg-hung rudder so she tracks well once we balance the sails. Under engine power, we can use the autopilot, but it drains the battery.

"That's great. If this wind holds, we'll be there in no time at all," I say between mouthfuls.

"Don't count your chickens before they hatch."

"I've ordered a wind vane to meet us in

Bermuda."

"You've wasted your money, this works fine."

"Don't you want to sleep yet? You've been up for more than twenty-four hours."

"I wouldn't," he says. "If I could have a couple of pints, I might, so don't nag me, woman, about sleeping. I'll go down when I'm ready."

We decided not to drink alcohol at sea. James agreed but I can see that it will be difficult for him to give up his favourite tipple.

I gaze out at the empty sea toward the horizon and feel my eyes relax as they adjust to the infinite distances of my surroundings. The blue sky stretches above us mirroring the ocean below. We are alone, in the middle of a blue universe.

"So, how did you find this boat?"

"I was in France, looking in marinas. I saw a photo on a website and right away I knew, this was the boat for me. It had everything I wanted on a boat. I called the broker. He wouldn't budge on the price because the owners just recently lowered it. I signed a contract by fax, sent in a deposit and flew to Florida on a one-way ticket. When I saw Eidos in real life, I knew I was right. Ken, the surveyor let me follow him around and ask all the questions. He even went up the mast."

I lean over the side and stare into the depths.

It's about fifteen hundred feet down and no longer recorded by the boat's depth sounder.

"Don't you think it's time to take that off?" James points to the Bahamian courtesy flag that flutters off the starboard spreader.

"You're right, we're now in international waters." I get up on deck, lower the blue, black and yellow flag, and then remove it from the clips. I can no longer see land.

I check the chart after putting away the flag. We are on course. The Gulf Stream current with its warm water surging like a river has Eidos in its grip pushing us north so we have to keep adjusting it slightly to the east.

"Take the wheel. The wind's up. I'm going to put a couple of reefs in the main." says James. "Don't want the mast breaking."

"You don't trust the rigging?"

"Not until we test it some more. I'd rather sail slower and get there. Remember the shroud that broke on Fenix?"

"I never had a survey done on her."

"Well, I don't trust it, and we're too far away from land if something happens."

He checks that the tether is attached to the D-rings on his inflatable life jacket at one end, and to the jack line on deck at the other, like a dog's leash to a clothesline. He releases the main sheet, then takes the end of the halyard from the cleat on the mast, lets it run free several feet, causing the sail to slide down, before cleating it off again. He then lashes the bulky fabric to the boom with ties. My job is to keep Eidos into the wind as much as possible without letting the jib luff.

"The GPS says we're still doing 5 knots, but now Eidos feels much more comfortable," I say. "I once saw a t-shirt that said, 'Sailing is the only sport where you can scare yourself to death going nine miles an hour.'"

"Let's just get there," James replies as he returns to the cockpit, dragging his tether behind. He unclips it from the lifeline and clips it the binnacle support.

At noon, I put away the chart of the Bahamas and open the small-scale one of the West Indies showing Bermuda near the top edge, and transfer our position from the GPS. I love to use paper charts and see our progress in small, circled crosses across the sheet. This also serves as a back-up of our position in case the GPS quits working. I fill in the next row of spaces in the logbook and then measure off our distance from Cat Island abeam.

"We're forty-five nautical miles from the nearest land," I call out to James. "And 700 miles from Bermuda."

"Don't scare me," he says. And then, "Hey, look over there!"

A small pod of a dozen bottlenose dolphins surface and dive, weaving their way through the waves half a mile from us, flashing their tails to the sky like needles poking through a turquoise tapestry. They come close and cross our bow, diving under the boat, turning their bodies sideways and watching us with one eye pointing up, as if to say, 'Hello!'

I rush forward to take a better look. James pulls out his video camera.

The dolphins follow us for several minutes before disappearing ahead.

"Wow! Hey, guys, so nice to see you!" I call out. "Come back!"

"Remember the whales we saw in the Sea of Cortez? Says James. "I wonder if we'll see some here too."

"You were always the first to spot them in the distance," I reply.

"It's my hunter's instinct," he says.

I smile and nod. We're friends again.

The colour of the Atlantic is a deep aquamarine verging on indigo with white foam near the boat where we gently slice through it. In the afternoon, two white arctic terns circle the boat for several hours.

"When I die, I want to come back as a dolphin or a bird," I say.

"When you die, you're dead," he replies.

I look out to sea, my eyes scanning its surface for more dolphins or whales.

We're still in the shipping lanes, and by evening, three freighters pass us in the distance and a tug with a tow gets too close for our liking. James calls it on the portable VHF radio and checks with its captain, who says that he will pass to our stern. I've heard that some big ships don't keep a 24-hour watch, depending on their radar to warn them, autopilot doing the steering. We don't have a radar, only a radar reflector mounted high on the port shroud. We hope for the best that they can see us.

Finally, at ten in the evening of the third day, James crawls into the quarter berth and is soon asleep.

I love the feeling of being alone while keeping watch, yet having the backup and the security of James below. It's unnerving to be away from land, especially when we see no other sign of human life. I try not to think about it. Eidos doesn't have a life raft, single sideband radio, or an EPIRB for any emergency. We are dependent for our safety on our vigilance, our skills, and the half-inflated rubber dinghy attached securely on the foredeck. However, I rationalize that people have successfully crossed oceans many years before all the safety equipment was available. I silently thank the Pardeys, Tanya Aebi, and Robin Lee Graham for their inspiration and guidance through their writings. Both Robin and Tania sailed alone around the world, when they were still teenagers and in smaller boats. If they could do it, we should be able to. And the Pardeys sailed without an engine and all the equipment that many people now need.

The sky is peppered with bright dots of light, the Big Dipper on the western side of the North Star. The moon lights the sea like an overhead lamp. It rises later now, at ten and has started to wane. It makes the night seem friendlier, warmer. The first time I saw a sky like this was during another voyage across the Atlantic when I was thirteen, immigrating from Poland to Canada with my parents, grandmother, and sister. Here, on board a small sailboat, I feel much more exposed and vulnerable yet awestruck.

It would be amazing to be one of the first astronomers on the ocean or in the desert, following stars, not roads to a destination. How fantastic to watch the celestial sphere and realize for the first time that the Big Dipper moves in a circle around one star while the rest of the sky moves east to west. I can easily understand why the ancient astronomers believed the earth was in the centre of the universe with a rotating sky above.

I double-check our latitude by measuring the angle between the horizon and the North Star with a protractor. Thirty degrees. To estimate the longitude, one notes the local time zone, which in the case of the Bahamas, is five hours behind GMT. Since the sun moves (or appears to move) three hundred sixty degrees around the world in twenty-four hours, then each hour, it seems to move fifteen degrees of longitude. In five hours it moves seventy-five degrees and so the Bahamas are at seventy-five degrees of longitude. It's a rough estimate but close enough. I know how to use a sextant, but with a GPS on board, it's hard to get motivated to take a series of sights and do the calculations.

I scan the horizon every ten minutes for any lights. There should be ships and other yachts heading from the Caribbean to Bermuda, but the horizon is empty. We are the only ones here, a speck in the centre of our own universe on an endless ocean.

5. *Drifting in Sargasso Sea*

If there is calm before the storm,
I do not doubt for a single moment that there will be peace after chaos.
-Sai Pradeep

Sunday, June 6.

In the morning, a few fair-weather, wispy mares' tails appear in the sky, suggesting high-level winds. The swell has increased to about nine feet, although according to the pilot charts, we're not supposed to have big seas here. Large swell usually predicts a storm.

"Mares' tails, it will be squally within a few hours," quotes James.

"The barometer is steady at 1024," I say as I

mark our noon position. "112 miles in 24 hours. 573 to go. Not bad."

All through the day, I keep checking the barometer.

Monday, June 7.

The wind is on the beam, the temperature mild, and the breeze light to moderate. The barometer is steady but the swell worries me. James focuses on keeping the boat sailing at her best. He feels more comfortable with the strength of the rigging now, so he raises the staysail, and our speed picks up to 6.2 knots.

I cook and bake bread, navigate, and keep watch when James sleeps. We are doing well, trucking along with Eidos eating up the miles.

Tuesday, June 8.

The wind eases and our speed drops to three knots. Tough luck just when we are getting excited about making a landfall. With only 230 miles left to go, we have entered the Sargasso Sea, a large area of the Atlantic famous for clear water, masses of floating seaweed and lack of wind. It is not possible to avoid it.

"We should motor the rest of the way, or we'll be here forever," says James, adjusting the flapping jib trying to coax it to life.

"Two hundred miles is a lot of fuel. That's hours of noise and smell," I counter. "The current is in our favour. I vote no."

"I want to get there."

"Let's wait a bit longer."

We contact Liberty Star, a 738 foot, 64,000-ton freighter we have noticed on the horizon, for a weather report to break our tie vote. According to the latest information, we're under the influence of the Azores high-pressure system that covers most of the Atlantic at this latitude. Winds are predicted to be light to moderate from west-south-west with a weak front.

"West-south-west winds are good for us."

We decide to keep sailing.

In the Bahamas, I had let it be known on the local cruiser's radio net, that I was looking for charts of Bermuda, the Azores, and the Mediterranean. Many people, who no longer needed their charts contacted me. Some of them expressed concerns about my projected voyage. They insisted that I should have a single sideband (SSB) radio, through which cruisers receive weather reports and routings from "weather gurus" and which can also be used to call for help when out of reach of the VHF stations. I heard that one of these radios costs about $3,000 by the time everything, including the antenna on the backstay, is fitted in place on one's boat. Not having that kind of money, and being a low techie, I had no problem resisting the pressure to get one. Someone even offered to sell me just the receiver for $100, so we could listen but not transmit. Once again, I said, "no, thank you." I had better use for a hundred dollars. Food, for instance.

During my stay, one of the self-appointed weather gurus presented a seminar for the cruising community in George Town. His purpose was to sell his weather prediction services to cruisers over the SSB. However, listening to him, I became even more convinced that for the expense and trouble it takes to get a forecast that's only valid for 12-36 hours and could change at any time, this did not make sense.

I've met people who are so focused on the gadgets on their boat it's a wonder they have time to look around and see what's happening outside. Instead, the captain fiddles with dials and levers to catch the correct station. Then he has to wait his turn until everyone checks in, which sometimes takes an hour. Finally, the guru comes on the radio with his version of the weather forecast. These predictions are often based on conflicting information and changing conditions. That's fine if it's something you enjoy and don't let the 'gurus' make the navigation decisions on board, but many people do, or the 'gurus' get upset if you don't. Who then is the captain of the boat?

I would rather spend the time preparing for a blow than listen to the weather report, which is only an intelligent guess when it comes right down to it. Most of the boaters we meet have way more money than I do, so can afford to buy the latest gadgets. I prefer to focus on the simple aspect of being one with nature.

Sailing in the Sea of Cortez in Mexico without an engine has taught us not to take the weather reports and the gurus too seriously. One time a strong, northerly wind was predicted, and we waited a week to sail. Finally, we left and had another two weeks of pleasant weather before the north wind finally arrived. In my opinion, the profession of a meteorologist is one of those jobs where you can be wrong half the time, yet still, get paid.

I remember reading The Long Way by Bernard Moitessier, a notable sailor who circumnavigated the earth via the four southern capes in 1968, in sometimes horrendous conditions. He used a tea towel as a hydrometer to predict the weather. Since he was using seawater to wash his dishes, the tea towel was full of salt. If it dried quickly, he knew the weather would continue to be fine, but if it remained damp, it meant a storm was brewing. James and I also wash our dishes in seawater. So far, our tea towel has been drying quickly.

And yes, if the swell increases or clouds gather on the horizon, I'll head away from that direction. But it is difficult to predict which way a storm will move and impossible to run away from one at five knots when it is moving at twenty. Hurricanes are notorious for changing their direction for no apparent reason and hitting an area that seemed previously to be in a safe zone. The "gurus" just put one more opinion on the table. I feel comfortable getting our weather forecast from ships we pass and James agrees. I always check the weather before leaving the harbour, delay leaving when severe weather is forecasted, and while at sea pay attention to the barometer and the clouds. And the tea towel.

Wednesday, June 9

Last night a flying fish hit the deck, and this morning I cook it for breakfast. It has a delicate taste, but James refuses to have anything to do with it.

"You've made the boat stink," he says.

"Feel free to use the head for bait, it would be nice to catch a tuna," I say.

"We'd be lucky with the gear you have. Besides, we'd need to be moving to catch anything. What about a swim?"

The sea is a deep blue and the few ripples sparkle like starlight in the sunshine. I can see down at least ten or twenty feet. I am tempted, yet feel anxious at the same time. We're over the Hatteras Abyssal Plain where the depth of the ocean is more than 16,000 feet. The only place deeper than this in the Atlantic, is the Puerto Rico trench at over 18,000 feet. It's a long way to go if you drown, but it's hot, and I haven't had a swim in over a week.

James lowers the swim ladder on the stern, and I put on my blue bikini and climb over the railing and down the four steps until I'm immersed in the cool, refreshing liquid up to my neck, only one hand holding on to the bottom rung.

"We're two hundred and thirty miles from the nearest land, and the water is nearly three miles deep," James narrates as he points the video camera at me. "Which kind of spooks both of us."

The water is as smooth as a silk bedspread and goes on forever. There is nothing around us all the way to the horizon. We are the only two people in the middle of this blue, vast expanse below, and underneath the immense, blue sky. The sun is beating down.

"Wow, this is amazing." I wish I had the courage to let go of the ladder.

We are towing an empty, white bleach bottle with a yellow cap on a yellow polypropylene line about 100 feet behind us, so if one of us falls off, we can grab it and pull ourselves back to safety. We call it the little puppy because it looks like a small snub-nosed dog on a leash, hopping on the waves behind Eidos. But I'm not a good swimmer, preferring shallow water where I can see the bottom beneath me, and hold on. I fantasize floating in the middle of the ocean with Eidos sailing away and James, with a smile on his face, waving from the deck.

"I'm afraid something will bite my leg."

"Go on, B, let go of the ladder."

I smile, but don't let go.

A school of triggerfish nibble on the bait of the fishing line that hangs below me, but none of them touch the rusty hook. If there are small fish around, there probably are bigger ones hiding under the boat, ready to attack their prey.

"There could be sharks under the boat," I say and quickly climb back aboard, shivering from just thinking of it. "Your turn." I grab a towel.

"No way, I'm not crazy like you. You'd leave me floating behind and sail away."

James ties the solar shower bag with a gallon of warm water inside to the mast, and turns the tap on the hose, holding it over my head, as I shampoo my hair, soap up and rinse.

He then flings the bucket on a string into the sea near the starboard shrouds and fills it. He pours the entire contents over his head and naked body.

"Brrrrr," he says and does it again before rinsing off with fresh water.

"You know, we're in the Bermuda Triangle right now. Ships and planes disappear from here under mysterious circumstances. That's why we haven't seen any. Woooo," I tease him.

At night, the stars fill the sky with their reflections on the smooth ocean below us. And so we continue to drift north in the centre of a universe full of stars.

The next day our noon-to-noon distance covered is only 15 nautical miles.

"We really should use the engine," says James.

"I like it here, the sun is out, we have plenty of food and water, let's enjoy sailing while we can," I reply.

"You mean drifting aimlessly. How big are the tanks?

"Thirty gallons of fuel and sixty of water. Plus the extra on deck."

"So, at one gallon per hour, we can motor for thirty hours. Minus what we've already used. Times five is 150 miles. Not enough to get us there."

"Let's use the engine for a couple of hours a day to keep the batteries charged. That will help."

I start the engine and turn the autopilot on. With the wind from behind, the cockpit and cabin soon fill with diesel fumes.

"Yuck. Have you ever had it serviced?" James asks.

I sigh. "I had it checked over and changed the oil and filters when I bought it in Florida. And then again in the Bahamas shortly before you arrived."

"It sure stinks."

I feel frustrated. There is always something to

do on the boat, and I can't do it all. I don't want to do it all. I wish there was someone to do it with me all the time, not just show up for the ride as James did.

After an hour, I shut the engine off. The batteries are fully charged, and we need to air out the cabin.

"We could try the drifter," I say. "I've never used it but maybe we could take a look."

"You have a drifter? Why didn't you say so before?"

"I forgot."

We bring on deck my lightest and biggest sail, a nylon cruising spinnaker in a forty-foot long nylon sock, and lay it on the deck and over the upside-down dinghy, forward of the mast, like a fat boa constrictor. James attaches the spinnaker halyard to one end and hauls it to the top of the mast, while I anchor the other end with a shackle near the bow and tie the sheets to the third corner. We raise the sock, using a thin line, the way a woman would pull off her stocking, revealing blue, white and red fabric which billows out like a captive balloon.

"Nice," says James.

We had a drifter on Fenix, my boat in Mexico because she didn't have an engine and the wind often died just before an anchorage, so this is not a new skill for us. But this sail is enormous.

There is only a breath of a breeze from the south as if Poseidon was blowing on his glasses, yet it is now pushing us at two knots.

In the afternoon we see another freighter, and I call the officer on watch. He tells us that the weak front has intensified and in twenty-four hours we're to get wind between 15 to 20 knots from the southwest with 8-foot seas and in forty-eight hours also from the southwest at 20 to 25 knots with 10-foot seas. Yikes! I begin to worry. Eidos hasn't been in rough weather yet. Although, with the wind coming from the SW, we should be able to go downwind under reduced sails. I've done this as crew on another boat in the Pacific, sailing on a long swell topped by curling waves. It felt exciting, like skiing down rolling hills.

The large swell and the mares' tails in the sky were our warnings of a gale approaching. There is nothing we can do about it except get ready. We douse the drifter by lowering the sock over it and loosening the sheets at the same time until it all looks like a large sausage hanging from the mast. Then James lowers it on deck and I stow it in the sail bag. James carries the sail bag to the forward cabin. I secure things down below, making sure nothing is likely to crash to the floor. James checks that the dinghy is tied down properly on deck. We adjust the steering whenever needed. The elastic cord is not working as well keeping us on course without wind but then we're not moving forward much either.

In the evening, the barometer drops to 1018, and by noon the next day, as predicted, we have wind from the southwest at 18-20 knots and seas 5-7 meters. Our speed increases to 4.2 knots on a course of 64 degrees and straight for Bermuda with 124 miles left. We should be there the day after tomorrow. Can we outrun the gale?

After the sun sinks into the waves and its last rays slide of the surface of the sea, I watch the ocean surrender to the night.

6. First gale

Friday, June 11.

I am awake. Something is wrong. Like a mother with a newborn, my senses are finely tuned to the small changes in Eido's rhythm even while I sleep. The boat is moving wildly, riding up and down steep seas, lurching and shuddering, tossing me around in my bunk.

My heart pounding, I crawl out, swaying as if I were drunk. I give the barometer a knock with my knuckle. It fell further still while I slept. The tea towel swings limply on a rail in front of the stove.

James, his face hidden under his rain jacket hood, steers from the cockpit while the engine rumbles.

Then I hear it – humming noise coming from

the bilge.

Every day, one of my duties is to check the automatic, battery-powered pump which is about the size of a fist, sitting an arm's length down at the bottom of the bilge at the foot of the ladder, in the lowest part of the boat. The pump is connected to a six-foot hose running back under the engine and then snaking up to a through-hull fitting above the waterline. Its job is to keep the sea and rain where it belongs – outside.

I lift the floorboard under the companionway steps. The pump is droning and slurping up the water, so it's not an emergency yet, but why is it on in the first place? And where is the water coming from? Possibly rain and hopefully not a leak in the hull. If it fails to keep up with the ingress, we're pretty much sunk. And yes, we could use the manual pump that's in the cockpit locker or as a last resort buckets, but not for long. The physical exertion of trying to empty water from the inside of the boat back out to sea would exhaust the strongest crew in no time at all. I make a note to check the pump every hour.

"We've got a leak somewhere," I call out to James.

"You're joking."

Eidos has eight through-hull fittings with

valves and hoses attached. That's eight holes drilled into the boat under the sea level. Two for the toilet (one for seawater intake for flushing and one for sewage outlet). There is another one to drain the sink. One more for the black water holding tank which we use in harbours and anchorages. There is one for the galley sink drain. One for the engine's cooling water intake and two for the cockpit drains. There is also a ninth hole where the propeller shaft exits the boat. This one doesn't have a valve to shut it off. I crawl back into the quarter berth, pull off the two small covers, switch on a light and peer inside.

The smell of diesel is overpowering as is the noise and heat of the running engine. The propeller shaft is turning as it should since James has the engine in forward gear. I carefully put my hand under the stern gland that seals the hull where the propeller shaft exits the boat. Water drips on it and I count. "One thousand, two thousand." A small amount of leaking is expected and necessary to keep the shaft turning and cool but it is leaking more than it should. That's one source. Water also drips from overhead, near a metal backing plate where the binnacle for the steering wheel is attached to the cockpit floor on the outside. The seal must have cracked. I make a note to check both in Bermuda.

I pop the two covers back in place and wiggle out of the quarter berth.

"Found it. Not an emergency." I explain to James what the problem is and he lashes some rope to both sides of the binnacle to keep it from wobbling.

I try to go back to sleep wedged in the quarter berth, but the teak cover over the engine compartment behind the ladder creaks and groans with the movement of the boat and drives me batty. Diesel fumes have made their way into the cabin and linger there unable to escape, just as I am not able to escape this hell on water.

I finally give up, put my rain pants, jacket, and life jacket on. Before crawling out from under the spray hood, I clip the tether to the life jacket D-ring. The other end is connected to the binnacle and its job is to keep me from falling overboard. In the cockpit, the wind savagely whips at our clothes.

We're 100 miles from Bermuda.

Saturday, June 12.

Sixty-four miles to go – speed 5.2 knots course 60 degrees. As the conditions get progressively worse, rain pelting down over the deck, we drop all the sails. There is no point in having them up. With waves almost as tall as the mast, when Eidos is in a trough, even with the third reef in and the jib rolled up to the size of a handkerchief, they flap annoyingly, ready to rip. When we are on top of a crest, they strain the rigging and heel the boat dangerously. We decide to motor to within VHF radio contact of Bermuda just in case we get in trouble. Bermuda Radio monitors the waters around the island and controls the harbour traffic.

When we get within 30 miles, we finally hear it, transmitting a weather update, but no one replies to my call. Even so, it is a relief to hear a voice from land. The forecast is a gale warning with winds SW 25-30 gusting to 45 knots. So much for the weak front.

Every half hour, I eagerly turn the radio on to see if Bermuda Radio station can hear us and to hear a voice from safety, our only link with land. I also make a Sécurité call to any vessel in the area with our position. This type of call is not an emergency, it is for information only.

"Sécurité, Sécurité, Sécurité. All ships, all ships, all ships. This is sailing yacht Eidos. This is sailing yacht Eidos. This is sailing yacht Eidos. Position 31 degrees, 48 minutes latitude north, 64 degrees, 43 minutes longitude west. Heading 60 degrees magnetic, speed 2.5 knots. Visibility zero. Possible shipping hazard. Sailing yacht Eidos out."

Since we have no radar, and visibility with the rain and the waves is limited to about half a mile from the top of a wave, we hope that whoever is out there can plot our position on their chart and avoid getting too close. Radar wouldn't be of any use here anyway with all the sea clutter – unwanted signals from the rain and the sea spray, confusing the picture.

But there is no response. This hopefully means there are no nearby ships to run us over. On the other hand, there is no one to help if we get in trouble. Yet, we are in a submarine exercise area, so I look outside just in case there is one nearby on the surface. But I see no flashing yellow lights, their identifying signals. Let's hope one doesn't suddenly surface underneath us.

The next weather report tells us that the seas will diminish during the next 24 hours and the wind will shift. The 15-20 foot waves surround us and rise halfway up the mast, steep and close together, more like black diamond moguls on a ski hill than rolling hills. I hide below, wet, cold, and shivering. James is battling it out in the cockpit. The rain pours in buckets.

By 04:00, we've motored several hours, and according to the GPS, are still 29 miles from land. Out here it could be two hundred and ninety for all that we can see.

Finally, at 10:00 and 26 miles from land, Bermuda Radio station responds to my call.

I switch channels from 16 to 27 according to radio protocol.

"This is Bermuda Radio, go ahead Eidos."

"Bermuda Radio, we are 26 nautical miles southwest of Bermuda. Eidos is a 32-foot sailing vessel. We've had rough weather, but all is well. It's good to hear your voice, Bermuda Radio," I say. Tears of relief well up in my eyes. The officer at the station thanks me for the call and asks me to call back when we are close enough to enter the port.

Bermuda has one of the most powerful radio stations in the world. The operators routinely put a radar tag on ships and yachts as soon as they are within 50 miles of the reefs and keep an eye on their course during the approach to the islands, so they likely knew that we were out there even when we couldn't hear them, but it still feels good to finally speak to a real person.

We keep motoring all day but with these waves and limited visibility it's not safe to enter the port by dark, so we resign ourselves to spending another night at sea. During my next call, the officer manning the radio tells us she doesn't expect ship traffic overnight, only possible yachts, so we don't keep watch. She also tells us to look out for the Gibb's Hill lighthouse on the southwest end of Hamilton Island, marking the offshore reefs.

The white flashing light can usually be seen 25 miles away, and there is also a red flashing light at five miles, which warns of immediate danger, but we see nothing.

It continues to pour. Eidos is lying-a-hull with all the sails down. We hide below where we are relatively dry and warm, and try to get some sleep.

Meanwhile, all night, just within reach, the lighthouse stands guard, warning ships of danger and its flashing light slicing the darkness like a sword.

7. Land!

The real act of discovery consists not in finding new lands but in seeing with new eyes.
The only adventure that is doomed from the start is the one we do not attempt.
-Paul-Emile Victor

Sunday, June 13.

Early in the morning, James calls me up on deck and points ahead.

"I can see lights flashing," he says.

"It must be the Gibb's Hill lighthouse," I check our position and the direction to where James is pointing. It could also be a ship's steaming or stern light on the horizon. I count the flashes. It is the lighthouse only seven miles away.

"Almost there," I say.

The wind shifts to the east, exactly from the direction where we need to go, so we continue to motor rather than tack back and forth in the 7-12 foot waves.

"I can smell land," I say.

James takes a whiff. "Rubbish most likely," he says.

"Not on Bermuda, it's civilized. One of the most expensive countries to live in."

"In that case, we're not staying long," says James.

"Good thing we saved the diesel for this last bit."

"B, if we had motored when I said, we would have been in the harbour way before the storm."

"You know we didn't have enough diesel. And what if we got close and then ran out of fuel? We could have been wrecked on the reefs." I take a deep breath and shake my head.

It could have happened. In the dark, with the rough seas, we wouldn't be able to see the land even if we knew where it was by reading our position on the GPS. Without the engine and with the southwest wind pushing us northeast, we could have been swept and wrecked right onto the ragged underwater rocks surrounding the island like so many ships have before the lighthouse was built.

But we made it across, and the wind eased just in time to navigate to the safety of the harbour.

"Look, James! Bermuda!" I call excitedly.

"Land ahoy," he yells out for the world to hear.

I can hear the relief in his voice and I am also giddy with happiness at finally seeing land again after ten days at sea.

As the day begins to lighten, the island rises faint grey from grey clouds among the grey sea, but soon turns solid among the liquid of the Atlantic while the clouds float aside to reveal the low-lying southern coast.

"There is the lighthouse!" I say.

Its white, tapered tower 117 feet tall and built in 1846, sits atop Gibb's Hill so that its height above sea level is 362 feet. It reaches to the sky and flashes its mirrors at the ocean. The red aviation warning flash at the top can be seen by planes from over 120 miles away at 10,000 feet altitude. From the sea, in good weather, ships can see its signal from 40 miles away. But during a storm, it is difficult. We didn't see it until the waves diminished.

We still have 15 miles to go northeast along the reefs while keeping at a safe distance in deep water, but the rain stops and the sun comes out. We see two other yachts heading in the same direction and wave excitedly. I can't help but wonder how close to us they were during the gale.

Bermuda Radio officer directs us to the entrance of St. Georges Harbour at the eastern end of the island and advises us to check in at the harbour master's office as soon as possible.

I raise our yellow Q flag on the starboard spreader to signal that 'my vessel is healthy, requesting permission to enter the harbour.' The flag was historically used to signal quarantine due to illness on board, but in modern times it announces that the ship is free of disease and requests boarding and inspection if necessary when entering a foreign country.

The noise of the engine is annoying, and it's a perfect day to be sailing, but we don't care, we will sleep safely at anchor tonight.

We pass a second lighthouse, St. David's and by four in the afternoon, reach the channel entrance buoy. The Town Cut, through which we must go, from the distance, looks very narrow between the two rocky outcroppings. So narrow, that not even two sailboats seem likely to fit side by side. But it's 250 feet wide, and cruise ships use it all the time.

I'm glad it's daytime and the wind is light.

"Help me find where we're going," I call out to James who is filming the old fort off our starboard side. I feel stressed on the helm, keeping an eye on other boats coming and going all around us and trying to follow the shipping channel navigational markers.

"Don't nag me, woman. You have plenty room." He shakes his head. "We made it, madam captain." He salutes and then points the camera at me.

I'm not sure I like being the captain. I depend too much on James. What would have I done out there during the gale had I been alone? I can't even imagine it. I realize how much I appreciate having his support and companionship, even though we often bicker.

Once inside the large, circular harbour, we head over to Ordnance Island and tie up at the customs dock, the same dock that bigger boats use. Luckily there are none here at this time, only two sailboats. The dock is several feet above the level of our deck and James has to fling the mooring lines around the posts.

We change our clothes and comb our hair to look presentable for the authorities. James climbs up first and then extends his hand to help me onto the dock. I feel wobbly on land, unused to its solidity.

"I feel as if I were drunk," I say to James.

"And I'm looking forward to my beer," he says. "Let's go, woman."

We walk toward the customs office and check in with our passports and yacht's documents.

"Are you the captain?" the woman on the other side of the counter asks as she looks at Eidos' registration and then at me.

"Yes, I am."

"Good for you," she says as she stamps my passport. "Glad to see a woman captain for a change." She checks the date on her stamp. "Welcome" - she thumps it on my passport and then on James's - "to Bermuda. By the way, do you realize that your passport is nearly expired?" She says to me.

"Wow! I hadn't noticed," I say.

"You can renew it in Hamilton at the consulate, but go right away," she says as she passes the passports back to us. "Your visa for Bermuda is good for three weeks."

"Oh, is that all?"

"Unless you have a major problem with your boat."

"Thank you, let's hope not."

Outside, James slaps me on the back and says. "Time for a beer." I heave a huge sigh of relief. We had sailed eight hundred miles, our longest passage together and it still feels unreal to be back on land.

We can't stay here, as this dock is only for checking in, so we climb back down onto the deck. I take the yellow Q flag off the starboard spreader and run up the Bermudian courtesy flag. By flying it, we acknowledge that we will respect the laws and sovereignty of the country we are visiting. James takes the mooring lines off the bollards. We move Eidos and anchor in Convict's Bay in the northeast corner of the harbour, among other yachts and close to the town. The name comes from the bay having being used in the past to house prisoners on decommissioned ships.

I look around trying to imagine it as it was in 1609, after Admiral Sir George Somers, to save his crew in the after-effects of a hurricane, deliberately wrecked his badly leaking ship, the Sea Venture, on the eastern reefs of the island. Over 300 ships have been wrecked due to these reefs that lie within 200 square miles of Atlantic surrounding the island of Bermuda. I'm glad Eidos avoided that fate.

We put the sail covers on and then relax in the cockpit with a well-deserved glass of brandy as we watch the sunset. I am exhausted but too excited to sleep. After dinner, I move some blankets and a pillow to the settee behind the table where I will sleep while we're in port. I sleep soundly without once waking up.

8. Bermuda

Monday, June 14.

Among the many tasks, we have two important goals to accomplish in Bermuda. First of all, I must renew my passport, which requires a trip to the capital of Hamilton. We also have to install a self-steering wind vane, which had been shipped from California. This is a wind-driven autopilot that will take over the steering job of the helmsman much of the time.

Besides that, I want to see as much as possible of this lovely island and we only have three weeks to do it all. Exceptions to the three-week visa are only made for yacht maintenance problems, crew illness, or if the weather forbids leaving.

After breakfast, we put the dinghy in the water and mount the outboard. Next, we fill it with two bags of laundry, our shower things, and ten days worth of trash. I climb in, James pulls the starting cord of the motor and we head for shore.

I want to tie up at the fancy-looking St. George's Dinghy & Sports Club, but James insists we go to a dilapidated commercial wharf, with nails sticking out from its rotting, wooden posts and planks.

"I'm not going where the snobby rich hang out in their fancy outfits," he says. "I like real people."

"The people at the club are also real," I say as I climb a rickety ladder. "They just wash and do their laundry more often."

"My point exactly," he says.

A man on the dock directs us to the laundromat where we stuff two machines with our clothes. Next, we find showers in a toilet block nearby. My first real shower in I don't know how long, probably six months, feels heavenly. I put on a clean dress and sandals for our first walk to town.

The closeness of everything is disconcerting and claustrophobic after having only the empty ocean to look at for the previous ten days. We walk down narrow streets, bordered by one and two-story, white, pink, blue, and cream-coloured houses and shops, amazed at the docked whale of a cruise ship looming over the white rooftops. We laugh, discreetly of course, at the Bermudian business people in their short pants with white knee-high socks and the pink-skinned tourists. James is now tanned, his skin tough-looking from the effects of the wind and sea spray, his hair a bit longer. I'm sure that I also look well worn in comparison to the islanders and tourists.

At the grocery shop, we buy fresh vegetables, some fruit, milk, cheese and eggs. I crave fresh fruit but prices are high. We locate the bus stop for Hamilton, our destination tomorrow. Finally, we return to pick up the laundry. Back on board, I string a line between the stays and the shrouds, and then hang the wet sheets, towels, and clothes, while James opens a can of beer in the cockpit.

Tuesday, June 15.

Early the next morning, back on land, we find the bus stop and head to Hamilton. I look out the window as we leave George Town, and zip past the airport on St. David's Island. We drive over the Castle Harbour via a half-a-mile long causeway that was badly damaged by Hurricane Fabian the year before, and which leads us to the Main Island. I make a note of the Crystal and Fantasy Caves, Tucker's Town, Bermuda Aquarium, and the Botanical Gardens, along the way, hoping we'll have time to visit them in a few days. An hour later we arrive in the capital.

We locate the Canadian Consulate in an unassuming three-story building across the street from the cruise ship docks. I fill out the required forms, and the clerk promises to send them by courier to New York since the Canadian Consulate in Bermuda cannot issue passports. Why not Ottawa, I'm thinking but don't ask. The clerk tells me to return in two weeks to pick up the new passport. She also promises to alert New York, that I need it quickly because of our three-week visitor visa limit.

We wander around the city and check out some of its attractions. The biggest ones are the Cathedral of the Most Holy Trinity and the city hall, but we are eager to get started on the self-steering project. We decide to put sightseeing on hold until Eidos is ready for the next passage to the Azores.

The Monitor wind vane that I had ordered in the Bahamas has arrived from California and waits for us at the St. George's Boatyard. Craig, the boat yard's owner, has been very kind to let me use the yard's address for the shipment, even though we will not be using it for the installation. He also paid the wharfage fee upfront, without which it couldn't have been delivered. I refund him the money promptly with a thank you. Bermuda is a duty-free port, so as long as the package is for "vessel in transit," there are no other fees and we have no trouble taking delivery of the five-foot cardboard box.

The bungee cord James tied to the wheel worked well in steady, moderate winds but not during the gale, so I'm glad I bought the vane. We load it into the dinghy and return to Eidos where I make sure all the parts are accounted for and begin reading the instruction booklet.

Over the next two days, having borrowed a rechargeable drill from another boater, James installs the vane on Eidos' stern, using the dinghy as a platform from which to work. First, we have to take off the boarding ladder and the dinghy davits to make room for the vane. The dinghy moves under his feet on the waves and is not stable enough to do a proper job.

"This damn dinghy. I can't do this with it moving all the time," he yells as he tries to position the support legs for the vane against the stern of the boat. "

"We could take Eidos to a dock," I try to be helpful.

"I've already started. You should have organized this earlier."

"I asked around, but we'd have to move the boat to Hamilton. There is no free dock space in St. George's."

"You should have had this done in Florida or the Bahamas, B," he complains. "I shouldn't have to be doing it."

"I didn't have the money in Florida, and in the Bahamas, it would have cost 25% more for duty."

"How much did you pay for this thing?"

"$4,500."

"I hope it works for that price."

He is right. I should have installed it in Florida in the boatyard where I bought Eidos but I didn't have the money and there were too many other things to do. Besides, I had an autopilot, and I only decided to head offshore once I was in the Bahamas. My son, Justin paid for it when I finally dared to ask him and even he said that he could have bought a second-hand car for the price.

I help as much as I can, but aside from holding the vane while he mounts it and passing tools, I can't do much else. After two days of work, the installation is not perfect – one of the support legs is out of alignment. By then, we are both fed up with working and with each other, yet there is still more to do.

"Thanks," I say as I put the tools away.

"I hope it works," says James.

We spend several days checking Eidos to make sure she is ready for the next part of the crossing – 1500 nautical miles to the Azores.

I clean out the water tanks, while James ferries containers of fresh water from the town quay with the dinghy and adds 60 gallons to the tanks. We shouldn't need to filter it from now on.

The engine is next. I change the oil and the filters and check for any leaks. Then we empty the deep cockpit locker on the port side, which provides the best access to the back of the engine. After removing a plywood panel separating the locker and the engine, I climb into the pit, scoot down under the cockpit floor and crouch behind the propeller shaft. I put my hand under the stainless steel rod where it exits the hull and count the drops of water that land on it. Two or three drops per minute are ideal, but I count more than a dozen. No wonder the bilge pump worked overtime during the gale. Inside the gland where the shaft exits the boat's hull, there should be enough room for it to spin but not too much. While the propeller spins, salt water gets inside, sprays over the back of the engine causing it to rust as well as filling the bilge. Using two wrenches at the same time to loosen the bolts on the fitting that holds the packing in place, I push it further inside the gland, to slow down the leak. While I am at the back of the engine, I also check the transmission oil and tighten all the hose clamps.

"That should do the trick," I say as I crawl out from the pit of the locker. We then replace the plywood panel and the rest of the gear in the locker.

Back in the sunlight, we pull all the cushions out on deck to dry and then James heads to town to do more laundry. While it's getting done, I clean the boat inside. On shore, James finds a used battery next to a dumpster, brings it back and hooks it up to replace one that is no longer keeping a charge.

We've been in Bermuda now for over a week and I'm ready for a break.

"Are we finally done?" says James.

"Let's go out," I say.

"Na, there is nothing to do here at night unless you spend a lot of money in bars," he says as he pops a tab on a beer can.

9. A couple of beer now and then

Alcoholism and probably drug or any other self-damaging addiction is a symptom of total rejection, conscious or subconscious, of values as they are sold to you or forced upon you. Alcoholism or addiction of any other kind is an act of self-defiance, but they are futile, because they are self-destructive. In this world, the only real act of defiance can be in art expressed. Any art even if it's only knocking a nail into a piece of wood, just as long as you are satisfied that it is what you have done yourself. Any art – even if it is only a prayer. And should this addiction persist after the cause of it is clearly recognized, then it is nothing more than a symptom of weakness... human weakness caused by fear. Fear caused by not realizing that fear is only the nether side of intelligence.

-Tristan Jones, Adrift

When James and I first met in Mexico, I had just left a man who was an alcoholic.

"How much do you drink," I asked him.

"Oh, a couple of beer a day," James said.

Well, it was only a couple of beer at first, but soon it became three and four. Beer was cheap in Mexico, 50 cents or a dollar a can, and so it was tempting to drink it instead of water, which was not always safe. I enjoyed it as well especially with a plate of nachos, but my limit was one.

"You said only a couple," I pointed out to him once.

"I have insomnia and need it to get to sleep," he replied. "Don't nag me, woman."

By then, we were half way up the desolate Sea of Cortez. We sailed well together and made a good team on board Fenix, but our relationship was never emotionally close. We always split all the bills and rarely went out. He was not physically abusive but I always felt hurt by the way he talked to me. Eventually, I went back to Canada and he returned to the UK. While in England, he looked after his sister and elderly mother and continued to travel abroad. There were other girlfriends but I didn't keep up with his news by then. Our communications became more and more rare until the day I decided to email him on the spur of the moment from the Bahamas. I guess I must have been desperate.

James brings beer on board and drinks in the cockpit from early in the afternoon until the evening. It looks to me as if he is trying to fill his own tank for the next part of the voyage. By the evening he is pretty much done for. I'm premenstrual. Bad combination.

"You're drinking again," I say.

"I only have to have a couple to help me sleep, B. You know this from Mexico, so don't nag me," he says.

"It's more than a couple, James. And it's only four in the afternoon."

"This is normal for the English, B. We're not prissy like you, Canadians. It's part of my national heritage," he says as he opens another bottle and raises it as if making a toast. "Guinness, the best beer in the world."

Judy Grisel, a psychology and neuroscience professor at Bucknell University in the U.S. and the author of *Never Enough: The Neuroscience and Experience of Addiction*, has dedicated her life's research to learning the root causes of addiction. She writes in Scientific American that 'some of us are prone to addiction because we are predisposed to especially appreciate new experiences.' She also says that 'from an evolutionary perspective, such tendencies may be a real asset... Society as a whole might benefit as novelty-seekers trail-blaze for us all.' According to her, addictive personality is one that needs and likes change and risk to expand and explore. This is important to evolution.

This would be James, considering his risky travel destinations and the need for alcohol. And perhaps me, to a lesser extent, since I prefer a natural high to alcohol-induced one. I am also quite aware of my tendency to call anyone who drinks more than I do, an alcoholic, while James doesn't think he has a problem.

"I want to do things in the evening, not just sit around watching you drink," I say.

"So go, I ain't stopping you. I ain't paying those prices in bars when I can buy it cheaper in a shop."

I'm reluctant to go to shore in the evenings alone, and there is really not much to do. Dinner and drinks perhaps or a movie. Alone. Again. In the Bahamas, the cruisers met on the beach for live music, cards, and crafts. Here, we don't know anyone. On board, it's difficult to read since at anchor we don't have much power for lights and

I'm too frustrated to see the solution of taking my book to a cafe on land. I end up playing solitaire by candlelight or going to bed early. Good thing, it's mid-summer and the nights are short.

James sits in the cockpit until he is drunk enough to be able to pass out. He crawls into the quarter berth and soon he's snoring. So now I can't sleep and get angry once again.

In the morning, I count eight empty bottles.

"You know, you can leave from here, and I could find another crew," I say to him one day.

"B, your face looks like a slapped ass when you complain like that," he says. "If you want me to go, I will, but you've got to pay for my flight back to the UK."

"I'm sure I could find someone here, the ARC Europe rally passed through, the Newport to Bermuda race boats will be here soon, and there might be other sailors wanting a change."

"You haven't much to offer to a man," he says. "This is no luxury cruise. You haven't any money, your boat doesn't have any of the toys most men want, and you're no spring chicken. Why would any other man want this? I'm the only one that will put up with you and this leaky tub."

I feel a stab deep inside each time he talks like that. He tells me it's the truth and calls phrases such as 'slapped ass' colourful language which he uses to describe his feelings accurately. I feel trapped. It's the responsibility of the captain to look after the ship's crew, even pay their medical expenses and repatriation if necessary. I don't have the money to pay for his flight, so he can be as horrid as he wants and I can't do anything about it. I get paranoid thinking that now he can even decide how long to stay and where we should go. I regret not getting him to sign a crew agreement upfront and getting a cash deposit for his flight home.

We enjoyed sailing together in Mexico and even at the beginning of this voyage when he doesn't drink, but alcohol turns him into an angry and belligerent man. Add to it the stress of having been together twenty-four hours a day for the past ten days under stressful conditions, and even people who have been happily married for twenty years could become enemies.

He may be right. Who knows if I could find another crew? I would probably have to pay for someone to help me for the rest of the voyage. Maybe it's better to sail alone, but I am terrified. Reading about other people who have survived storms at sea, I believe that Eidos can handle the voyage. *Perfect Storm* story by Sebastian Junger was a good example. The crew of the sailboat panicked and called for a rescue, yet the little boat, similar to mine survived. When I first considered buying Eidos, I emailed Ted Brewer, the designer and asked him whether the boat was strong enough to sail offshore and he replied yes, it was and that usually, the crew was the weak link in any voyage. What I am afraid of is getting hurt while alone too far from any help. At the deepest level is my fear of dying alone.

The only time that I sailed alone overnight was thirty six-hours along the coast of Florida from Fort Myers to Key West right after I purchased Eidos. Most of the time, I was within hailing distance from Coast Guard's help if needed. It was tiring because I was close to shore and worried about running aground so I couldn't sleep. But in the middle of the ocean, it is possible, and some people sleep all night. I would need a radar detector that would wake me if there was a ship in range. But I can't deal with the possibility of getting seriously hurt or falling overboard with no one there to help.

"Look B, we made it this far, let's not quit now," says James. "We've done all the jobs, so now we can relax a bit."

James calls the woman he knows in Bermuda.

We invite her and her boyfriend for a visit on board. I am relieved to hear that she has a boyfriend, which makes me realize that I still have some feelings for James and worried that he might flirt with her in front of me. But no, they are only friends. Before leaving, Brenda offers us the use of her scooter and gives us a list of local attractions. What a way to see the island!

We tour the islands for three days and James eases on his drinking. He handles the scooter like a pro, weaving in the traffic with skill. We ride from Fort St. Catherine at the eastern end of St. George's Island to the Royal Naval Dockyard and the National Museum at the western end of the Bermudian archipelago. We stop at beaches and parks along the way, visiting the two lighthouses of St. David's by the airport and Gibb's Hill, such a welcome sight after the gale.

"I'm afraid of heights," says James. "You go, B and take some photos for me from the top."

"You? Afraid of something? That's hard to believe. I had no idea," I say.

"Well, you don't know everything about me," he says.

I climb the 185 circular steps of 19th century Gibb's tower and take in the view of the many islands and anchorages as well as the reefs surrounding Bermuda. Hundreds of yachts dot the blue sheltered bays.

While we tour the islands, we talk to people we meet and learn that the previous September, Bermuda had been hit by a hurricane with winds of 150 miles per hour and waves reaching 35 feet. Four people died while crossing the causeway near the airport because of a storm surge. We are lucky not to have experienced anything like it so far but I get nervous – it's now the end of June and the beginning of the hurricane season in the Atlantic.

I get a pleasant surprise once we return to the anchorage. A couple I had met in the Bahamas are now also anchored in Convict's Bay. Bill sailed with a crew and stopped in the States along the way, and his wife, Maryanne flew in for a week's visit. They invite us on board, but James refuses to go, and I am glad. I have a lovely reunion dinner on their boat, Owaso. They ask me what my family thinks of me sailing across the Atlantic.

"My sons are very supportive," I tell them. "They're grown, of course. They say, do whatever makes you happy, Mom. Ryan is an engineer, just married and living in Taiwan. The younger one, Justin writes video games for a living and came to visit me in the Bahamas," I tell my hosts.

"And your parents?"

"I didn't tell them. They want me to go back home and live a 'normal' life."

"I can understand why." Maryanne nods with a wry smile.

Being on board Owaso and getting treated well makes me realize how unsuitable for each other James and I are. With Bill and Maryanne I relax and laugh, something I never do with James. I wish I could invite my friends to my boat, but I worry that James will be drunk and embarrass me. Before I return to Eidos, we promise to keep in touch.

At the end of two weeks, my new passport arrives, and we go back to Hamilton to pick it up. I want to stay another week to see more of the surrounding reef area, snorkel, swim and explore the natural beauty of the islands, but James wants to keep going. He is impatient to get back to England.

"I promised my girlfriend, I would be back in six weeks," he says.

"I had no idea you had a girlfriend," I say. "You never told me."

"You don't know the half of it."

He doesn't say anything else and I don't pry.

We do a last shop for provisions and top up fuel and water. James heaves bags of groceries on the side deck and I stow them down below: potatoes, onions, oranges and cans of tuna and stew. Bermuda is expensive so we can't buy a lot. I'm running out of cash.

"You sure this is enough food to get us to the Azores?" Says James.

"I still have some rice, beans and pasta left," I say. "Let's hope the Azores are cheaper."

I check my email one last time but there is nothing from my editor. Finally, we take the dinghy to the harbour master's office and check out.

10. Good bye Bermuda

June 27.

We ease out of the Town Cut in the afternoon steadily and comfortably, leaving a stream of white sea foam behind us. Under cerulean skies, a light southwesterly breeze persuades the unfurling jib as I shut off the engine.

Once clear of the reefs surrounding the island and past a cruise ship heading north, I adjust our course to east by northeast. This direction, according to Jimmy Cornell's World Cruising Routes, will take us to 40 degrees north latitude, where the wind is good and steady.

Before long, Eidos is sliding down the waves at four knots, while St. George's Harbour and Bermuda fade away under the sparse clouds in the peach coloured, setting sun. Our next destination, Flores Island in the Azores, is almost 1700 nautical miles away, so we should get there in about three weeks. This is more than double the distance we have sailed from the Bahamas.

I hope we can outrun any bad weather. I hope nothing breaks. I hope neither of us gets hurt. There is always a risk of injury on a boat and away from medical care, it is much more important to stay safe.

Please look after us, Poseidon.

While James is on watch adjusting the self-steering vane in the cockpit, I go below deck and unroll the small-scale chart of the Atlantic. The Azores is a tiny sprinkling of brown dots on the right side of the mostly white sheet covered with blue depth contour lines. I run my hand through my hair and take a deep breath.

The barometer reads a healthy 1025 millibars of pressure, the sea rolls lightly ruffled from behind us, the sky is partly cloudy. The forecast predicts much of the same for the next four days, with the wind rising to 20 knots. To the north, a front has formed while a high-pressure system, with light winds, takes over most off the north Atlantic to our south. Tropical outlook: storm formation not expected. I check the GPS display.

"Hey, James," I call out of the cabin.

"What?"

"We're sailing at 3.6 knots or a brisk walking pace."

"Are you trying to make me feel better about this damn trip?"

Why so slow? In these conditions, we should be moving at least at 5 knots. Are there weeds and barnacles growing on the bottom of the hull? I should have checked.

Monday, June 28

We sail following the band of gentle winds in between the stormy front to the north and the windless high-pressure system to the south. If we get too much wind, we plan to head southeast, and if not enough, we will sail northeast. Right now we are too far south because the wind has almost died, but things should soon improve since our course is northeasterly.

But things don't improve. The sky grows grey and the sea follows, erasing the horizon between them. Below, a steel grey, oily-shiny sea surrounds us with a trim of white, foamy breaking waves near the hull like epaulets on an officer's shoulders. Above, a lighter grey sky and white clouds. We are in a world that has turned from Technicolour into a black and white movie. Soon the rain pitter-patters on the deck above me as Eidos rocks and rolls on the waves. I brace my left hip against the icebox to steady myself while buttering bread in the galley.

"Pass me my rain gear," James calls out.

I hand him his red Gortex jacket and pants, and from the safety of the cabin, scan the sky behind us. A massive wall of steel-grey clouds threatens along the horizon as far as I can see. Bright swords of lightning explode between the clouds and the sea. I count one, two, three, and then thunder shatters the silence with a reverberating boom. A knot tightens in my stomach. We are the only tall object for hundreds of miles around. I put the portable GPS and VHF in the oven for safety. I wish I could crawl in there too. The last weather report didn't mention anything about thunder and lightning.

"I thought it was summer," I whine to James. "What's with this weather?"

"I don't mind, it's only water," he adjusts the clutch between the vane and the steering wheel. "I think I've got this figured out now."

It's a good thing we have the self-steering vane. It uses wind for power to hold us on course and gives James more time to rest and hide inside when it rains.

"I like our third crew member," I say. "It doesn't eat or drink, doesn't get tired, and doesn't complain."

"Oh, yes, it complains," says James. "Can't you hear the squeak as it adjusts course?"

"It needs a name, so I propose we call it Squeaky."

Now, one of us only has to pop a head out of the cabin every ten minutes to check the horizon for ships.

We eat vegetable soup for lunch but soon after he's finished, James goes out again.

"Why aren't you staying inside?" I ask.

"I don't feel well."

"Seasick?" Eidos is rolling around in the swell.

He nods without saying anything and looks out toward the horizon. I follow his gaze. Anchoring one's eyes on the horizon usually helps to steady the stomach, but there is no horizon with all the grey. I'm usually fine, having lived on the boat for so long but it still takes a few days to get our sea legs. We don't like taking medication for seasickness and prefer to tough it out eating lightly and drinking lots of water.

At three in the afternoon, I check our

position. In the first twenty-four hours, we manage to cover 58 nautical miles on the rolly seas. Not a good start. We have 1640 miles to go. Luckily, the storm doesn't get any closer and stays in the north part of the sky.

Finally, James reaches his endurance limit and lies down to sleep on the cabin floor where there is the least motion.

"Downwind sailing is overrated," he says. "Not bad when the seas are flat and we have the drifter up but this is shite."

"I agree," I say. "On a reach or close-hauled she just trucks along."

Tuesday, June 29

In the morning, the clouds move to the horizon and the sky is mostly clear. The sun pokes its orange, coral and pink head out of the cobalt sea which is lightly ruffled as if covered by a wool blanket. Its light floods our world and edges the fluffy cumulus clouds with a trim of crimson lace.

James wiggles the binnacle that supports the steering wheel and the compass.

"B, the bolts holding this thing down are loose. Try to tighten them from below."

I grab a wrench from the toolbox, slide down

the quarter berth, open the inspection ports and try to tighten the nuts. One rusty bolt breaks off and falls into my hand with its threaded nut. There are three equally rusty bolts left holding up the binnacle. I don't dare to try and tighten them. I show the bolt and nut to James.

He shakes his head. "What else, B?" What else is going to break? I thought you had this boat surveyed."

I drop my head down and shake it. "You know, I did. Water must be getting in under the binnacle base and dripping down the bolts."

"Pass me some wire or rope." He makes a brace from the binnacle to a spinnaker winch using a wire-coated cable.

"Do you even have an emergency tiller?"

I open the cockpit locker and show it to him lashed to the side.

"Have you tried it?"

"No. I never needed to."

He checks its length. "I'd have to take the wheel off, but it might fit."

Perhaps James could also adapt the wind vane connections to the tiller, but it would get complicated.

"Your boat is a complete wreck," says James. "You should have done more work to get it ready for this trip. I wish I had never come."

"This is part of the risk of being out here," I counter. "Even new boats have problems. If you had read some books, you'd know this."

"And all you know is from books, which is dick all."

I feel safe, as I've already sailed on Eidos for the past eight months and know that whatever happens, we can handle it. I trust James' skills and determination as well as mine. I only wish he'd stop complaining and getting angry.

Sailing solo once again becomes tempting. Alone across the ocean is more about the mental aspect than the physical. Tanya Aebi did it, and she was only seventeen. I could do it and in the worst-case scenario, heave to and wait out bad weather. But mentally, I am not so sure. It is really good to have someone to talk to and bounce ideas off, even if we mostly argue. I suppose we could turn back to Bermuda for repairs, but the jury rig is holding for the moment and so we continue on.

Wednesday, June 30

"Whales!" shouts James as he points to the southern horizon.

"Where, where?" I scan all around me. James

is always the first one to spot whales and dolphins. He says it's his hunter's instinct.

"Over there," he points shaking his arm.

An enormous, grey head of a humpback whale rises out of the sea. It launches its giant body with a great whoosh out of the waves, completely clearing the sea in a tremendous breach. After a moment of seemingly being suspended in the air, it crashes back down on its back. Another whale follows, and then another, and another.

They are merely a quarter of a mile away from our cockle shell, Eidos.

"Wow," I cry out. "I hope they don't come any closer!"

Whales have been known to sink boats. If one of them landed on the barely eight-ton Eidos, its 25 or 30 tons would surely sink us. There have been incidences of whales sinking yachts, one of the more notable ones in the Pacific. Dougal Robertson and his family were sailing between the Galapagos Islands and the Marquesas when their yacht, Lucette, was attacked by three killer whales and sank in less than five minutes. Six people, including two children, survived for 38 days in a life raft and dinghy before being rescued. Having read their story in *Survive the Savage Sea*, I know I don't want to add that kind of experience to my list of goals.

But every spring, approximately 12,000 North Atlantic Humpbacks migrate from the Caribbean where they breed and have their young, north as far as Iceland, to feed all summer, so the risk is always there.

"In my next life, I want to come back as a dolphin or a whale. It must be wonderful to be so free." I gush. "Isn't this worth it? Doesn't a moment like this make up for all the cold, rainy nights and boat problems?"

"Only if we survive and after we get there," James admits reluctantly. And then he smiles.

In Mexico's Sea of Cortez, we had a curious mother and baby grey whales swim right under Fenix, our tiny sloop, while we drifted on a calm day. We loved sailing slowly without an engine as it allowed us to hear the whales' exhalation spouting out of the sea even before we saw them.

Today, the whales keep away and gracefully swim and dive, soon disappearing from our view.

The wind picks up just when I begin mixing the ingredients for bread. It's like getting rain right after you've washed your car or watered the lawn. It's pleasant to sit in the cockpit in the warm sunshine, kneading the dough, and it rises much better without a cooling draft. However, we do need to get there and need the wind but we're still only managing three knots.

"If we could do 100 miles per day, we would be in the Azores in 16 days," I say as I tuck myself under the spray hood with a bowl of dough in my lap and a wooden spoon in my hand.

"At least now we're moving." James is fiddling with the vane again. It has trouble steering downwind and tends to wander from side to side.

"It's all this side-to-side we're doing instead of forward. Either northeast or southeast but never in the direction we need," I say as I step down below, flick the pilot light on in the oven and put the dough in to rise.

At noon it rains again. I collect two litres of water in a bucket tied to the mast where the rain flows off the sail. We have plenty in the tanks, but have to be careful and have shut off the tap on one tank. This way, if the water is contaminated in one, we can still use the other one. I strip down, grab a bar of soap and climb up on deck by the mast. Just as I get soaped up, the rain stops, and I have to use the water from the bucket to rinse off.

James is trying his hand at fishing. "Let's see if we can catch anything on this rusty hook." He shows me how to set up the fishing line. Fresh fish would be good to add to our menu of canned tuna.

We have to pay attention that the safety line we trail behind with the bleach bottle tied to it, our little 'puppy,' with the pink nose, doesn't get tangled up with the fishing line.

"We're not going fast enough to catch anything," he says and then hauls in the line.

There is lightning all night again in the distance and I keep a wary lookout, but the storm doesn't get any closer and I feel thankful.

11. The drifter

It had long since come to my attention that people of accomplishment
rarely sat back and let things happen to them.
They went out and happened to things.
-Leonardo Da Vinci

Thursday, July 1.

The wind is light today, so we carry the drifter sock from the fore-cabin and hoist our lightest sail. It billows out like a giant bubblegum bubble and flies happily pulling us behind, getting our speed up to 4 knots.

"Maybe we'll make 100 miles today," says James.

"That would be amazing," I say.

But suddenly, just as we relax in the cockpit, enjoying a second cup of coffee, the whole sail collapses and drops into the ocean, splatting itself like that bubble gum bubble exploding on one's face. Eidos sails over the nylon sail before it slows down.

"Bloody hell!' exclaims James. 'Bloody hell. What now!"

I run forward and grab the part of it still attached to a sheet, pulling the soaking fabric out of the sea so it won't drag under the keel.

"Come and help me," I shout to James. The sail is heavy with pockets of water trapped in its folds like a giant squid.

"You can do it, B. You don't need me."

I heave and pull, and drag and struggle, and finally, a mass of nylon is laying on the deck, on the top of the upside-down dinghy, and tangled around my feet. I check the head of the sail. It is no longer attached to the halyard.

"What happened?" James asks.

"The halyard knot undid itself, and so here it is," I say. I look at the mass of rope on top of the dinghy looking like a nest of snakes.

"Are you sure you know how to do a bowline?"

"I thought you tied it off."

"Well, what do you expect, I'm not a sailor," says James.

"Help me with this. I want to hang it to dry."

"You can't, it will fly away." James is watching me from the cockpit shaking his head.

He is right. He passes me a sail bag, and I begin stuffing the wet mass of the sail and the snuffing sock into it, but it's unwieldy, and I'm struggling.

"Help me."

"I ain't helpin you, B. It's your boat, your problem."

I resume the struggle, crying with frustration. I'm soaking wet, the sail is heavy with water and gets tangled between the stanchions and the deck hardware. I wish I could strangle James but instead, I'm being strangled by the sail.

Finally, it's in the bag, and I tie it down on the deck. I untangle and coil the halyard.

"Well, that's great," says James. "Now we don't have a light air sail."

"What did you expect? A cruise on the Queen Mary?" My frustration turns to anger.

"I thought the boat would be in better shape. I thought it would be rougher and faster. You said it would only take six weeks and now it looks like it will be longer."

"But it's you who insists on reefing the sails all the time," I counter.

"Would you rather we lost the mast overboard?"

I suspect he is argumentative because he is missing his drinks in the afternoon and suffering from withdrawals but say nothing. No point making him angrier than he is already.

We see dolphins later on but this time they don't come close. Shearwaters skim the surface of the ocean, flying near the dolphins marking a school of fish below. A large fish launches itself from the depths to get away from the predators. James and I don't speak for the rest of the day.

The boat is falling apart and so are the remains of our relationship.

Friday, July 2.

I'm glad I no longer have to be out in the cockpit all night, only every ten minutes to scan the horizon because it's raining again, and it's cold. Much colder than on our previous passage. We are nearing latitude 38 degrees north. The wind picks up, blowing from the southeast which is on the nose again, the seas increase to four feet with white caps. Our speed increases to 4.5 knots under the main alone. James worries about the rigging again, and he thinks we can go just as fast with the second reef in. I don't mind and he puts it in.

I make the usual fried potatoes, onions, garlic and egg frittata for breakfast and split pea soup for later. James eats whatever I put in front of him. Most of the day, while the wind vane steers tirelessly, we sleep or read. No ships and no whales to worry about.

When the rain stops, I hoist the spinnaker on the staysail halyard to dry. James still refuses to help. The fabric is soaking wet, stained with rust bleeding from the metal fittings and it looks awful. My beautiful sail ruined. I should have dried it yesterday. It would have been so easy with help, and I struggle to lay out the nylon parachute fabric on deck by myself, while the wind is blowing it all over the place flapping it wetly over me. I end up crying and feeling sorry for myself.

I need a man to do things with. A good man, where is he, God, why do I always get stuck with the mean and nasty ones? Please send me a good man.

Finally, I give up and stuff the still wet drifter back in its bag. It's a good thing the wind has increased so we can't use it anyway.

I eagerly wait for 15:00 when I calculate our 24-hour distance covered. So far we've gone only 294 miles in four days – not as far as we had hoped but not bad. The wind has been fickle and often dies down at night. We only manage about 3.5 knots of speed heading downwind. Eidos would go much faster with twin jibs poled out on both sides, but we're worried about the strength of the rigging. Besides, I don't have any poles, and we're too far from land to risk breaking something else.

I go below and check the barometer. The arrow on the instrument has moved toward the left to where it says, I knock on the glass cover to reset it then open the logbook and fill in the spaces on the page. Barometer: 1024 MB. Seas: 4-5 ft. Wind: 15 knots. Wind direction: SE. Sky: Rain. Under notes, I write: Starboard tack. I plot our position and measure the tiny distance on the chart of the Atlantic. Distance covered. 55.7 NM. I draw a sad face in the log. I wish I could write 100 instead.

In the evening, the rain eases, and the clouds thin to the east, letting the moon poke its head out from behind them now and then. It's full for the second time during our voyage, but this time it's pale and offers little light.

"Hello there, Mr. Moon," I smile for the first time in a long time. "So nice to see you even a bit."

Like a street lamp on a rainy, autumn night, the moon makes the night less threatening, less cold. The nights are now getting longer each day, but I am no longer lonely. I love the emptiness of the ocean and sense a greater presence all around me. I shiver in the cold of the early dawn.

James usually sleeps for the second part of the night, so I'm alone for as long as I can stay awake. He does a longer stretch during the day and late into the night because I do all the cooking and navigating. He tries to catch up on sleep during the day but doesn't seem to need as much as I do.

I could do this alone. Perhaps slower and with less sail up. Now that I have the wind vane to steer, I would only need a radar detector to watch for ships while I sleep. James is not doing all that much out there, just adjusting the wind vane now and then and mostly complaining. He hasn't helped with the drifter, I had to get it out of the sea and stuff it into the bag. I do all the deck work, I do all the navigation, I cook. And yes, it's nice to have someone to talk to but if that's all...

When I look back over my past thirty years of sailing and cruising, the number of times I have sailed alone adds up to a very small percentage. Short day sails, mostly. The reason for that is partly because I like to sail with friends, but mainly out of fear – an unfocused fear of the unpredictable great ocean. Perhaps it is the pack instinct. Being alone is inbred in us as being dangerous.

According to Mihaly Csikszentmihalyi, professor of psychology at the University of Chicago and the author of *Finding Flow*, the word 'Idiot,' originally meant someone who lived (and perhaps sailed?) by himself. 'It was assumed that cut off from community interactions such a person would be mentally incompetent.' Csikszentmihalyi also says that 'in contemporary preliterate societies this knowledge is so deeply ingrained, that a person who likes to be alone is assumed to be a witch, for a normal person would not choose to leave the company of others unless forced to do so.' Or couldn't find crew.

But then came my first overnight sail alone. I had just bought Eidos. I had a deadline to leave Florida for tax reasons (and yes, I know, a calendar is the most dangerous item on board a boat) and could not find a crew in time. I needed to get from Marco Island to Key West on the west coast. About ninety miles. The water along the coast is very shallow, with only a narrow buoyed channel. I was afraid of running aground and not being able to get off, more than I was afraid of deep water. So after agonizing about it for a few days, with my heart in my throat, I pulled up the anchor and set out.

I decided to head out for about four hours and then if I felt brave enough to go on, I would. If I lost my courage, I still had enough daylight to get back to the anchorage. All went fine for the four hours and at the point of no return, the weather was pleasant, with light wind so I was motoring, the autopilot was steering and I decided to keep going, pleased with myself.

However, an hour after the point of no return, King Neptune decided that I needed a lesson in rough conditions. The wind increased to 15-20 knots and the seas rose to 5-7 feet. I had to go on because not only was it too late to turn back but also the wind was from behind and if I turned around, I would have had to beat into it, which would involve being out overnight. At that point, my autopilot quit, overworked by the rough conditions so I had to steer by hand.

So there I was, alone, about 20 miles offshore, since the coastline recedes as you head south, steering by hand and too frightened to go on deck and raise the sails. This was not a day sail. I knew I was one level up.

The night came and my fear increased. I

could not see anything. No land, no ships, not even a light. By then I was exhausted. I wanted to sleep badly and nodded off now and then. But soon I would be jerked awake. I peered into the darkness, expecting to be either run down by a ship or overwhelmed by a monster wave. It was the longest night of my life.

Finally, when daybreak arrived I could have cried with joy. My reward came when a pod of dolphins found me and played around Eidos. Following the channel to Key West anchorage required that I pay attention when I was the most tired. By the time I arrived in the anchorage I had been up for 36 hours. In a daze, I dropped the anchor and slept.

The next day, James spots our fourth ship, heading to Gibraltar and asks for the weather report. The officer on watch tells us: wind from the south, force 5-6 which means up to 27 knots. But there are no major weather systems anywhere.

"I'm happy we can manage without an SSB radio," I tell James. "It's so easy to get a weather forecast from the ships. This gives us a reason to call them, so they know we're here in case they're not looking."

"Yeah, those rich people can keep the radios,"

he replies. He is not a gadget man, preferring machines, the bigger, the better. When he travelled to Australia, he found a job on a farm driving combines.

In the afternoon we play scrabble and James wins by 100 points.

12. Ocean wide, ocean deep

Sunday, July 4.

Most of the fresh food is gone, so from now on, we will be eating pasta and rice with some mangy potatoes, onions, and eggs to break the monotony. We also have a few cans of stew, beans, and tuna left in case we run out of propane for the stove. And bread, our mainstay, always and also as long as the propane lasts. Our favourite food, canned mandarins, were too expensive in Bermuda, so we don't have any of those on board. Today it's beans and eggs with bread for breakfast. For lunch, I am having a bouillon cube broth with noodles and James with rice. I could eat more, but we have to ration ourselves in case we get into trouble. I also have to drink more water, so I don't get dehydrated, but it tastes and smells of bleach. James put too much in when filling the tanks in Bermuda. I hope it doesn't make us sick.

"Is that the second piece of bread, B?" James asks me as I chew on the second piece of bread. I give him a dirty look and stick my tongue out. "I am being careful. But I have to eat. You're the one that could eat less, you have more fat to lose."

"Well, don't eat it all."

I am hungry. If I can't eat enough to keep my energy and my body temperature up, we will be in survival mode with one crew member hypothermic and unable to take her watch. North Atlantic is much colder than the Bahamas and we have been eating more.

Later, when he is in the cockpit, and the hatch is closed, I open a can of tuna and skulking on the heaving floor in the dark, eat it with a fork straight out of the tin.

The barometer has dropped over the past three days, slowly at first then faster – three millibars in 24 hours. It looks like we'll be getting another gale. The wind is blowing from the south at 25-30 knots, seas are 6 to 7 feet high, and the sky is slightly overcast. We're sailing on a reach, Eidos' fastest point of sail. If this continues, in twelve more days we should reach our landfall, Flores

Island, the most western of the Azores chain. Knock on wood.

Monday, July 5.

The waves grow, and Eidos rides over the top of most of them, but now and then she gets a wallop on the side and over the deck. I hope the wind moderates soon. Eidos is sailing well under staysail alone.

But James is not happy. "Go and tighten the staysail halyard B," he says. "The sail is too baggy."

"I tried, it's too hard for me. Why don't you go?"

"You can do it, just use the winch."

"James, it's a five-minute job for you and fifteen minutes for me. Why do I have to do everything?" I whine like a child.

The staysail has to be pulled higher, and while its boom is loose, it could bash me on the legs or head. I suppose if I were alone, I'd do it. Or perhaps I would leave it until the wind died.

"Because it's your boat," says James.

I refuse to move, and so he flings the staysail sheet off the cleat and lets it bash around making the sail flog.

"You'd bite off your nose to spite your face," I

yell at him and duck back inside.

Let him deal with the sail.

We get a gorgeous sunset tonight, spread over the western horizon like a bloody stain.

"Red sky at night, sailors' delight," I say.

"I sure hope you're right," says James.

Tuesday, July 6.

By morning the seas are still lumpy, but the wind has shifted to the west. The sun clears the horizon, blinding us with light that shimmers on the surface of the water. The sky is tropical blue. What a difference the sun makes. I smile as I click my camera in all directions. This ocean is huge--so much water and the nearest land is over 500 miles away. On and on it goes. I'm in awe of all this magnificence. We've seen no ships, no birds, and no whales for four days. And only us in the middle of it all.

In the afternoon, I bake brownies.

"Don't use all the propane, B," says James. "I don't want to eat cold stew for the rest of the trip."

"I guess you don't want any more brownies then?" I move to take the plate back inside, but he grabs it and laughs. "Just be careful," he says.

I wish he was in love with me, but even in Mexico, I felt that he was guarding his heart and just using me. Of course, now I was using him, so perhaps we're two of a kind.

At three in the afternoon, my time to plot our position, we are almost at 37 degrees north, the latitude of Flores Island. All we need to do from now on is head directly east. We are still in the grip of the Gulf Stream but it is much weaker and cooler here. At night I put on all my warm clothes yet still shiver. Every ten minutes, I poke my head out, check to see if our wind vane, Squeaky is keeping us on course and take a look around the empty horizon for any lights indicating ships nearby. There are none.

Thursday, July 8.

This morning I notice a ship on the horizon and turn on the VHF radio.

"Big ship, big ship, big ship, this is Eidos," I repeat while pressing the transmit button on the microphone. I then give our location and request for the weather forecast, but there is no response. The ship looks like a navy destroyer, so we're not surprised by the silence. Most of the officers on watch on board all the ships we've seen have been reluctant to chat even if they respond in the first place. Perhaps because we don't call the ships by name. Perhaps they don't want to be diverted to some sailboat needing food or fuel and thus be late arriving at their destination. I can understand that, so that's why when I call, I give our position and request a weather update before anyone answers to put their minds at ease that they won't have to take more than five minutes out of their busy schedule on board.

As on most mornings, we shake out a reef from the main, unfurl the jib all the way out and are soon moving at nearly 6 knots. James watches the rigging for signs of problems, but I'm happy we're making miles. We always reef for the night just to be on the safe side.

We are almost halfway to the Azores with 840 miles to go. This is the farthest I've ever been from land. We have a glass of brandy to celebrate and a granola bar. Pasta for lunch. The seas are growing again. The barometer is still high at 1028 and wind from the south at 16 knots. A perfect day. The current is pushing us south since the GPS shows that Eidos is moving at 115 degrees and the compass shows 90 magnetic. That's 25 degrees off. I check the pilot charts and yes, the Gulf Stream angles south in this area. It could sweep us off course unless we keep an eye on it and adjust our heading.

Saturday, July 10.

The barometer starts dropping again, heralding bad weather. We notice a container ship on the horizon and heading in our direction. When it gets closer, I note the name on the hull.

"Sealand Achiever, Sealand Achiever, Sealand Achiever, this is sailing vessel Eidos. Sailing vessel Eidos. Sailing vessel Eidos." James calls on channel 16 of our VHF radio.

"This is Sealand Achiever," the officer on watch replies. "What is your name and position?"

James reads out our latitude and longitude coordinates and asks for the latest weather report.

"There is a low between 40 and 50 degrees north and 50-70 degrees west heading ENE," he tells us. We are at 38 degrees 15 minutes north, 47 degrees 05 minutes west. It is right behind us heading in the same direction.

He then asks us if we need anything and where we are headed.

"Thank you, we're doing fine. We're on our way to Flores Island," says James.

"Best of luck to you," he says and signs off.

There is no way we can escape the low while sailing at four or five knots. I suppose we could head more south. It's a trade-off. Turn more south and get less wind and away from our goal, or go for more wind, more speed and more directly on course for our destination. We'll just go for the rhumb line now. The wind is southerly 10, so no worries at the moment.

Sunday, July 11.

It is a grey day, heavy with clouds and only small bits of blue here and there. No rain so far today, but it did rain last night. The decks are wet. The sea is smooth with some occasional white caps. We hope to find the east-going current near here. The wind is still from the south. Eidos is galloping across the waves.

The main with a second reef works well to about 18 knots of wind at which time James puts in the third reef. We have the jib rolled up partway to balance the sails and ease the helm. The Monitor is happy making very small corrections. Our little white puppy with a yellow nose, on the yellow polypropylene rope, makes us laugh as it hops over the waves about 100 feet behind Eidos. All it needs is two eyes, and our rescue line float will really look like a puppy on a leash.

13. Close encounter and a second gale

Monday, July 12.

We had a rough ride last night on choppy waves and according to the chart, we're over the top of a 2,000-foot undersea mountain chain, the North Atlantic ridge and a volcano with 5,000 feet of water on top. This area is prone to earthquakes which can cause tidal waves. An earthquake or a volcanic eruption might have caused the chop because the wind is light. I wouldn't want to be here in a storm. The shallower water will boil up as the surrounding seas have to pass over the undersea mountains. They come to the surface forming islands such as the Azores. Perhaps the struggle is over, we're over the top, and it's going to be a downhill ride from here on. The Azores islands belong to Portugal, so we'll be in Europe when we get there.

We've also reached the latitude of the east-flowing current and Lajes on Flores Island. Let's hope we're on a moving sidewalk for the remaining 575 nautical miles. We could be there in five days if the wind holds.

All day and night, as usual, every ten minutes, we scan the horizon for ships. After finishing my watch, I go down to sleep, and James takes over.

Wednesday, July 14.

I wake up and in the light of early morning, see that James is lying down on the settee. It's his watch, but his eyes are closed. Thinking that he's tired and not wanting to wake him, I get out of my bunk and start climbing the ladder leading into the cockpit to check for ships.

"I just looked five minutes ago," he yells after me. So he is awake.

I go up anyway.

"Oh my god, come and take a look at this!"

A huge container ship is passing us about 100 yards away, pushing a massive bow wave in front of it. Eidos begins to rock on the swell. I stare at the ship dumbfounded.

"But I just looked," says James. He is standing behind me on the companionway steps.

We are frozen in silence as the ship barrels west. There is no one on deck, and I don't see anyone through the windows of the bridge. It moves on like a phantom. The distance presses the ship further and further into the grey clouds like a thumb pushing it into putty until it is absorbed by the horizon and in ten minutes it disappears as if it was never there. We are stunned.

"It must have been in my blind spot," says James.

I look to the east. The rising sun, low on the horizon shines into my eyes. The ship came from there.

"Do you want to call them and ask if they saw us?" James goes out in the cockpit to scan the horizon.

"No." I'm still shaking.

It's too late to call, the ship is gone and what would they say? Probably that we should have been watching for them. I turn the radio on, but there is no one there. I don't get mad at James, I am in shock, grateful to be alive. A slight wind shift for us or a tiny course adjustment of the ship's autopilot and we would not be here.

"We should keep the radio on all the time,"

says James.

"What about the batteries, will it not drain them?"

"I'll make sure it won't."

I take a deep breath and wait for my racing heart to slow down.

If I was sailing alone, I would have had a radar detector. It would have beeped and warned me. I thought that having a crew was enough. So now we have to make sure to take a good look around rather than just a brief scan. We saw four ships in the past two days so we are definitely back in the shipping lanes.

Besides the actual ships, we also need to watch out for containers that fall off them. An estimated 2,000 to 10,000 containers are lost at sea each year. Most of them eventually sink, but until they do, they could inflict major damage to a yacht. They are difficult to see among the waves, especially at night and if they are partially submerged like icebergs. Yachts that sail fast are at a bigger danger than Eidos, which moves at an average of only 3 to 4 knots. I check the GPS display. We're doing 6.5 knots.

That afternoon, another navy ship from the Netherlands looms on the horizon. We get a weather report predicting stronger winds rising to

25 knots, perhaps a gale, with decreased visibility in the next 48 hours, which will last for four days. Less visibility means more danger of getting run down.

We are keeping the VHF on now all the time. I pick up the microphone and make our presence known. Another sailboat, a 56-foot yacht, Monterey, is 16 miles away to our south and moving at nine knots. Compared to Eidos at 32-feet, the other yacht is almost twice the size and much faster than we are. Our visible horizon is only about two miles, so we never get to see them. They tell us that they left Bermuda seven days ago, to our sixteen. At this rate they'll be in the Azores in about 24 hours and before the gale.

At night, I make a general Sécurité call every half an hour to let other ships know our position, so they don't run us over. I am exhausted but keep setting the alarm. James is in the cockpit keeping watch. We can catch up on our sleep during the day.

Friday, July 16

Two days later, the weather improves. A faint rainbow graces the sky to the southwest. I stare at it in wonder as it stretches across the sky behind us. My eyes are starved for colours other than blue and grey.

Eidos is now gripped by a current that's pushing her south instead of east, so to counter it, we have to sail into it otherwise we get swept sideways. We have 200 miles to go. Two more days, if we could go faster. I start the engine, and we motor sail for an hour.

In the afternoon, we finally lose the current, and our speed briefly picks up. But then the wind changes direction, rattling the sails and slapping the halyard against the mast. It begins its ghostly moan and quickly increases. For the hundredth time, we adjust the sails. Then it starts to rain, and the wind dies.

I hide inside while James is on watch.

We must have a leak somewhere because the cushions are damp again. The deck is fibreglassed below the teak, but perhaps it's all those hundreds of holes where the screws are keeping the teak attached that are letting the water in. Or the bolts for the chain-plates are working loose. We'll have to dry everything when we get to the Azores. I huddle in a corner of the quarter-berth where the cushion is still dry.

The wind, waves and current continue to conspire against us coming from the northeast – the direction where we want to go. We're back to the third reef in the main, and the jib is almost completely rolled up, so of course, we're not moving forward, only up and down, a motion that shakes the mast and the boom. Squall line after squall line thunders over us, spitting out bolts of lightning. Eidos is lifted to the top of every boiling crest and then sent careening down the trough. We need to charge the batteries, and so James turns the engine on and we motor into the waves and make some slowly won miles. I hide inside where it's warmer and safer. In 24 hours we make 45 miles. If we could walk on water, we'd get there faster.

By evening, the wind is still howling with the sea heaving halfway up the mast, so I go on deck and pull the main down, while James rolls up the rest of the jib. It's pitch black all around with only Eidos' navigation lights glowing eerily in the sea spray so that big ships hopefully can see us. The barometer needle is still sliding down.

In the cabin, I pick up the VHF microphone, press the transmit button. "Sécurité, Sécurité, Sécurité. This is sailing yacht Eidos, Anyone out there?"

14. For want of a shackle

July 17.

I am nearly asleep, wedged crosswise in the quarter berth. The ocean tosses Eidos around like a cork. James is in the cockpit running the engine. There is no point in sailing, the waves are too big, and the wind is on the nose. The steady drone of the engine is hypnotic. Its teak cover where I've braced my feet is creaking like old woman's bones, and the smell of burning diesel fills the cabin.

Clang! Grrrrate. Boing.

I sit up and hit my head on the overhead ceiling.

"What was that?" I'm now wide awake, my heart pumping. I jump out of the bunk and lift the floorboards above the bilge pump. It is silent and the water is at its usual level. I heave a sigh of relief.

"I don't know. Maybe we hit something." James puts the engine in neutral and looks behind the boat. "I can't see anything here." His voice is unsteady.

I scramble back into the quarter berth and open the two engine inspection ports – nothing unusual there. We wait for something else to go 'boing', but nothing does. James cautiously puts the engine into forward gear again. All seems well but going to sleep is now out of the question. My mind is spinning. There has to be a reason for that horrible noise. James comes down below, and I take over the watch.

"What could it have been? Did we hit a drifting container?" I ask.

"It sounded like something hard and metallic hitting the prop," says James.

"So a container?"

"Or your anchor. We've been moving up and down a lot in these waves and you didn't secure it like I told you."

I nod. It could be the anchor but it's too dark and rough to go on deck to see anything right now. It will have to wait until dawn. I spend the rest of the night in the cockpit, my ears piqued for anything else to go wrong.

Finally, daylight arrives and I peer forward. It's difficult to see over the dinghy lashed on the foredeck, but if I stand on the edge of the boat, on the teak coaming, first making sure my tether is clipped in, holding on to the swaying boom and stretch as high as I dare, I can see. It is the anchor. Or rather, it isn't there anymore. My best anchor, the 25 lb CQR is no more. I feel sick to my stomach.

In the Bahamas, James had suggested I shackle the anchor to the bow roller. He didn't think that the pin through the shaft attaching it to the roller was strong enough. I forgot to do it. It slipped my mind. Now, that slip has caused the anchor to slip into the deep blue. Fifteen thousand feet of deep blue.

When James wakes up, I tell him the good news.

"I told you to put a shackle on," he reminds me with a wry smile.

"I know, I forgot." I stare at the floor, thinking about what to do next. I put the engine in neutral, clip my tether to the jack line and crawl forward along the starboard side. The deck is heaving underneath my body while I focus on the next handhold that will stop me from being flung into the sea. The rode is still hanging over the bow roller. A wave crashes against the boat and it soaks me to the skin. But the news is good. The anchor is still attached to the boat. The pin came out of the retaining hole, the anchor jumped the bow roller, 85 feet of chain followed and then 200 feet of rode. I open the chain locker. The plywood bulkhead dividing the two chain lockers is damaged, but there is hope. The end of the rode is still attached to the D-ring inside. All we need to do now is pull it all back up.

"It's still attached," I yell over the noise of the engine and the wind.

"Cut it off," James replies from the cockpit. "Or it will pound a hole in the boat. Or the bowsprit will break, and if that happens, the forestay will go and so will the mast."

I check the foot-long bowsprit that supports the anchor roller and where the forestay is attached at the aft end.

"It seems fine. It has a steel backing plate." I counter. Two stainless steel rods also support it from underneath. They don't seem to be damaged.

"I'm not pulling it all up. Cut it off," he insists, holding a rigging knife in my direction.

It is a lot of weight to haul up 200 feet of rode, 85 feet of chain and 25 lb CQR from the depths. That's more than 100 pounds. I have no windlass, only manual cockpit winches. I refuse to give up. There has to be a way.

"This is my best anchor, and we need it for the Azores," I argue.

"What about the other one?"

"It's not very good, and has only 30 feet of chain and not enough rode."

I grab a length of a mooring line, then hang over the edge of the boat at the bow and tie a clove hitch from its end to the rode as low as I dare. I then lead the mooring line through the fairlead to the starboard bow cleat. Once it's secure, I cut the rode inside the anchor locker to relieve the strain on the bowsprit, the forestay, and the mast.

Now the strain is on the cleat, which is strong. The other end of the mooring line I lead down the deck to the cockpit winch but realize that I don't have the strength to take it off the cleat. Besides, the clove hitch is not going to fit through the fairlead.

Using the same system of tying a clove hitch with a second mooring line onto the anchor rode, I lead it outside of everything to the cockpit winch, put three wraps on the winch and cleat it off. Next, praying that the clove hitch will hold once again, I take off the first mooring line. So, now the anchor rode is perpendicular to the cockpit winch with only one way to go – up, instead of up at the bow, and then along the side deck. I start cranking. With a two-speed winch, the rode moves up about an inch every rotation of the handle. I begin to sweat. This will take a while.

"You'll never do it alone," says James.

I keep cranking. It's coming up but very slowly. I need a man or a block and tackle, but I refuse to ask James for help. It should be obvious what's needed. He finally realizes it'll take me several hours of hard work to haul the whole thing up.

"Shift your fat ass," he says.

I get out of the way and James grumbling and swearing begins winching. I breathe a sigh of relief and tail with as much force as I can muster.

For the first time in a long time, I look around. Eidos is still getting tossed by the waves. It is grey and dismal and with not much visibility. Who knows if there is anyone else out there. I haven't made a Sécurité radio call for several hours.

Finally, the chain reaches the coaming. James keeps cranking. I cringe as it chews up the teak decking outboard of the winch as well as the drums on both sides. We are now using both winches for safety, but at least the anchor is coming up. James is not straining as much, so there is progressively less weight to lift.

Finally, the anchor clears the surface of the water.

"Yeahooo, we did it!" I holler.

"All this for a stupid anchor," he says.

"Sorry. Thanks," I mumble.

James heaves the anchor inboard and places it on top of the rode and chain piled on the floor of the cockpit. We are exhausted, but we won.

The anchor, chain and rode will have to stay in the cockpit for the remainder of the passage as it's too risky with the sea so rough to move it back to the bow. We take a break, and then I make a big breakfast even though it's the middle of the day. The rescue had taken all morning. In the afternoon, James raises a reefed main, and we continue sailing toward Flores Island.

In the evening, James starts the engine to charge the batteries but as soon as he puts the gear into forward, the engine grinds to a halt.

"What the hell."

He puts it into neutral again and looks behind the boat.

I follow his eyes. Our little puppy bleach bottle with its yellow floating line is nowhere to be seen. I look down over the stern rail and notice that it is still there, but very close to the hull and the yellow rescue line is tangled near it. It seems that while we were hauling in the anchor and the chain with the boat in one place, the stern of the boat lifted out of the water on the waves at some point. The floating man-overboard line that we always trail behind, wrapped itself around the rudder and the prop.

"I guess you'll be going for a swim," says James.

I laugh. "No way. I'm not going into that water. I can't see the bottom. I bet you sharks are hiding under the hull."

Once when I was snorkeling in Mexico I saw a barracuda bigger than my leg and didn't relish a repeat of that experience. James is not any braver than I am, so for now we have to be careful when using lights and the radio since we can't charge the batteries without the engine.

The wind eases, while the clouds trimmed with deep red, brood on the horizon to our stern. Red sky at night, sailor's delight. The gale has ended. We shake the reef out of the main, unroll the jib and point Eidos toward Ponta das Lajes lighthouse on Flores Island. Its pinpoint of light pierces the dusk as Eidos aims for it like an arrow heading for a target.

15. Flores Island

July 19.

The sea is kind to us as we near the volcanic islands of the Azores, smooth and gentle underneath Eidos' hull. It is early in the morning, and James is the first one to see Flores.

"Land!"

"It's beautiful," I say, laughing. We slap our hands together in a high-five. The most westerly one, Flores Island looks like a black cloud in the distance but soon becomes solid with the sharp edges of the mountains showing against the dawn sky. James pulls out his camera and takes a photo of me with the sun behind.

We watch as the globe rises out of the sea next to the island's profile, deep red turning orange, and finally covering the sea with its yellow light. The mainsail and the jib are fully out to make the most of the light wind. Without the use of an engine, we need to be careful but the wind is steady. As we get near, my eyes bathe in the green of the hills that are dotted with white dwellings near the edges of the clay cliffs steeply rising out of the sea. We haven't seen anything green in three weeks. I had no idea that I could miss something like colour.

We follow the island's jagged cliffs, like teeth along a jaw bone of an enormous shark waiting to devour us as we sail into its open mouth late in the afternoon. Eidos drifts into the shelter of the anchorage on a dying breeze. There are a few other yachts in the anchorage, so I choose a clear spot, and then turn the boat into the wind. As the mainsail begins to luff, I pull on the main sheet to bring it in and roll up the jib while James takes off the shackle securing the anchor to the bow roller and lowers it into the water. We had moved it, the chain and the rode from the cockpit back to the bow yesterday in preparation and I made sure that this time it was securely attached.

We have sailed into anchorages dozens of times on Fenix, so it's as if the manoeuvres are in our blood. It's calm inside the wide bay, and we can't dig the anchor in without the engine, so we have to trust its weight and the weight of the chain to hold Eidos in place. James pulls the mainsail down and lashes it to the boom.

"We're home!" I call out as I let go of the wheel and raise my arms to the sky.

"Time to celebrate," says James.

"I better check the prop in case we need to get out of here in a hurry and need the engine," I say.

I'm not looking forward to it, but I don't even bother asking James to do it. I already know his answer. I put on my bathing suit, then my snorkel and goggles and climb down the ladder into the sea.

"How is the water?" asks James.

"Colder than in the Bahamas," I answer, and then take a deep breath and lower myself as far down as I can.

Yes, the yellow polypropylene line is wrapped around the propeller shaft several times. James passes me a knife, but the rope comes off easily just by pulling on the end. James pulls the bleach bottle and the loose line out of the water using a boat hook. We were lucky the line didn't weld itself onto the shaft of the propeller, or we could have had serious damage.

I also check the hull for barnacles, but there is only a light coating of slime on the surface of the bottom paint. I had cleaned the bottom in the Bahamas, and the anti-fouling paint is still doing its job keeping the critters off that would slow us down.

"The bottom is fine," I call to James. "I think we're so slow because we're always sailing with one reef in."

I climb back out and rinse off in fresh water on deck. Next, I turn the engine on and carefully put it in reverse to dig the anchor in. All seems to be well. Finally, we can relax.

Sitting in the cockpit, we enjoy a glass of brandy as we take a look around. The water in Lajes Harbour is clean, but it is a working seaport with commercial vessels tied inside the concrete breakwater and sea wall. The Azores used to be a major whaling centre since the islands lie on a migration route for several whale species. The wide bay of Flores is open to the east. Squat, red-roofed houses crowd its steep shore. Several yachts are in the anchorage, but it is not busy.

We move our watches three hours ahead to fall in with local time. We've been sailing on Bermudian time for the whole passage, and according to our watches, it's been getting light earlier in the morning and dark earlier in the evening, but I didn't mind, it made the nights shorter and warmer. Yet, I wasn't bothered by early dark in the evening when dusk arrived at six. It was in the morning after a long and cold night that we needed the encouragement of the sunrise as early as possible. And so over 1700 miles from Bermuda to the Azores, we lived in our own time, as well as our own place in the universe.

On Flores Island, it isn't difficult to adjust the watches to a new reality, the bigger difficulty lay in walking on land, the different space reality. The land seemed to be moving under our feet, and we were wobbly and dizzy at first. I was also disoriented by the middle distance. On the boat, you live in the immediate distance and look at infinity. On land, the infinity is chopped up by the middle-distance objects such as mountains, hills, and buildings.

Communication is relative too. Both the Bahamas and Bermuda use English as their main language. But now, all of a sudden, we are thrust among people who don't understand us and we don't understand them. We practice our simple Portuguese, memorized from a phrasebook, and have no trouble getting what we need. People are the same everywhere – we all need to eat and find shelter. When we arrive at the anchorage, most people around us know why we're here, they know we have sailed from far away, they know we are probably tired and relieved at having arrived. This gives us a common link to other cruisers and the community, although separated by language and space, we are nevertheless very close in spirit.

July 20.

James helps me pull out all the cushions on deck to dry, then lowers the dinghy in the water. I fill it with our trash, empty water and diesel containers, and the propane bottle. We don't bother with the outboard and James rows us to shore.

As we climb the 600-meter hill to the town, I notice the sharp volcanic rocks. The Azores Archipelago was formed by a group of undersea volcanoes, part of the ones we passed over a few days ago. The houses of the village of Lajes are scattered on the rocky hillside.

"Ola," they greet us as we meander up the streets looking for the Port Police. A man points in the direction of a building, knowing exactly where we need to go without us asking. We check-in and receive a poster stating that we have crossed the Atlantic. Not quite yet, but almost.

The library is next – to send emails to family

and friends telling them that we are safe. Finally, we buy a few provisions and return to the boat. Tomorrow we'll explore the island.

For the next two days, we hitchhike around Flores taking in all its beauty. High mountains crowd the tiny island, steep and rugged. Stone walls cut up the pastures beneath their peaks, and stone houses with red roofs dot the landscape. We admire the tall waterfalls, and pristine, steep-sided deep lakes filling ancient craters. Flores Island is an island of flowers. Hortensia, red and purple, cannas and wild roses edge most of the roads and cover the stone walls. There is an old harbour in Santa Cruz protected by a natural rock formation, but it's too small for yachts. A few fishing boats rock on their moorings. The preferred harbour for yachts, where we are, is in Lajes, even though it is open to the northeast and ocean swell.

I'm glad James is with me. I wouldn't have dared to hitchhike alone. Perhaps if I had stayed long enough, I would have made friends with the locals or other cruisers. Maybe I would have been adopted by some local family and shown around, but it is good to have a man's presence. When I've sailed alone, many people ask me where my man is. Why don't you have a man? There are so many single men wishing for a woman to sail with. They don't understand why anyone would live on a boat alone.

They make it sound like it's my problem and perhaps it is. Yes, there are plenty of men to sail with, but they haven't asked me out. Perhaps they're intimidated by an independent woman. James isn't intimidated but then nothing fazes him. He crews for me and I offer him an adventure that he wouldn't get otherwise unless he joined a male captain on his boat. I ask him why he hasn't done that.

"I wouldn't put up with a male captain on his boat. With you, I am the captain without the hassle of boat ownership. I like to be free."

James is eager to get moving again. Before leaving Flores, we pick up some groceries and top up our water. Prices are much lower than in Bermuda, so we stock up well. James secures the binnacle with a new bolt. We don't talk about the drifter which lies soggy in its bag in the cockpit locker. We lift the dinghy back on deck and go to bed early.

16. Horta and Sao Miguel

July 23.

At daybreak, while I start the engine, James hauls the anchor back on board and secures it with the new shackle. Our destination is Horta on the island of Faial, 117 miles away. One or two days. It's nothing compared to our last passage. The sky is grey. There isn't much wind, so we motor for awhile charging the batteries. I am glad when we finally shut the engine off and sail. I love the silence and peace of the ocean away from land. I can breathe and relax and I'm glad to be away from people, noise, shops, cars. Out of the corner of my eye, I notice a dark shape near the boat.

"Dolphins!" I call out to James who is

adjusting the wind-vane to steer us in a straight line.

He tries to film them, but they're elusive, diving back and forth under the boat.

He is quiet today, not his usual self.

"Are you OK," I ask.

"I just want this thing to be over," he grumbles.

"You don't like it?"

"It's taking too long."

"I've been enjoying it. Especially once the engine is off and the weather is calm."

"We're going too slow."

I like having someone to share things with, but I wish he was enjoying this voyage more and not only as a means to an end. I could stay out in the middle of the ocean forever if the weather was warm and the wind gentle like we had for a few days out of the Bahamas. Trade winds. We planned to sail around the world on the trade winds once.

And of course, I wish he was more loving and kind to me and not so abrasive. Most of the time I feel hurt, insulted, criticized, or ignored by him. We seem to be on different wavelengths. 'We're chalk and cheese," he once told me.

When we were a couple, even sex was

impersonal, just a way to relieve tension. We are missing an emotional connection that I long for with a man. Yet, I believe that deep inside, like everyone, he needs to feel loved and his abrasiveness is just a way he tries to protect himself from being hurt. This is why I usually forgive him for the way he treats me. Today, he seems to be a little more friendly.

In the afternoon, the sun finally comes out from between the clouds and we are sailing on smooth seas.

It feels like we're on the home stretch. The last downhill run after a full day of skiing. As if all the storms and cold weather are behind us. I know that's not true, yet, I begin to look forward to finally arriving in mainland Europe.

The sun makes all the difference in my outlook on life. That's another relative thing. On a cloudy day, I have less energy and feel depressed. On a sunny one, I feel alive and happy. In Victoria, on the west coast of Canada where I lived for 20 years, most of the winter was cloudy or raining. When I left for work it was nearly dark and after spending the entire day in an office under fluorescent lights, by the time I got home, it was dark again. I felt like I was a mole hibernating, waiting for life to begin. On the rare clear days, the sun was pale, anaemic, seemingly struggling to shine.

One winter, I lived in the mountains at a ski hill village, which was in the valley and so it was dark all the time, except in the middle of the day. I never saw the sunrise or sunset, hidden behind the mountains. I would ride the gondola to the top of the mountain as soon as I could after my early morning job selling tickets, and ski the upper part of the mountain soaking up the light.

That's when I decided to live near the ocean and as far south as possible. My sons were living with their father by then.

I sailed to Mexico as crew and there, I felt fully alive and never depressed. A friend who lived in Canada told me that she used an infrared lamp for 45 minutes each day to help her body adjust to a lack of sunshine in winter. How sad, I thought, while I was sailing, where the sun shone most of the year.

"I'll never live where I have to wear socks again," was my mantra for the many years that followed. But I don't belong in Mexico. I belong in Europe where my roots are and southern Europe because of the sun. We were almost there.

By nightfall, we have 50 miles left to go. The wind increases to 20 knots from the northeast and we are right on course. The sea is getting rough, so James reefs the main and I roll up the jib part way. I begin to worry about how we're going to enter an unknown harbour in the dark with rough seas and strong wind. We decide to ride out another night and plan for our arrival in the morning.

July 24

The sun rises out of the ocean, shimmering orange through the waves. James is awake, so I hand him a mug of coffee, put a Mozart CD in and switch the cockpit speakers on.

"Turn that off – I hate opera," he says.

I turn the CD player off and tell myself, soon I will be on my own, have patience. He spoils everything and adds another nail in the coffin of our nearly dead relationship. I thought he might change but the longer we are together, stuck like this, the less I like him. Even when he doesn't drink, he is mean.

I check the chart to make sure we're still heading in the right direction, but now it's easy to see where our next harbour lies.

The island rises steeply from the ocean. There

is an old volcano in the centre. Snow white houses topped by red roofs nestle in a sea of green vegetation. The capital itself sits in the lap of an amphitheatre of cultivated hills.

The town of Horta with a population of about 15,000 inhabitants is a popular stopover for yachts. It was first settled in the mid-1400s by Portuguese farmers and traders. Because of its location, it became a convenient stopover for North American whalers as well as merchant ships on the trade routes to the New World. Now instead of whalers, cruising sailors fill its harbour.

We arrive in the early afternoon. The marina is very well protected behind two breakwaters and is full of visiting yachts. We manage to secure a berth and tie up. Faial is the most popular island in the Azores for yachts because of the safe harbour as well as the murals that the crew of every boat that passes through here paint on the sea wall or the concrete quay. I admire them as we pass other cruisers on our way to the marina office.

I want to paint Eidos' name on the harbour wall as well, but don't have money for paint and I don't want to do it alone. Everyone else seems to be with someone, either a crew or a partner. I don't dare ask James for help. He would probably laugh at me and criticize people defacing the stonework with their so-called art. He speeds up and is soon out of sight likely heading for the nearest bar. I feel lonely. I walk slowly along the docks and the sea wall hoping someone would talk to me. Everyone seems to be having a good time chatting while they stir the paint in the cans, add finishing touches to their creations, comparing their work with others. I feel left out and miserable.

"Hi, Barb," a nice-looking man smiles and waves a paintbrush at me. "Remember me? I am Steve. We met in the Bahamas."

He is crouched next to the wall, surrounded by several cans of paint. He is touching up the blue sky above a sailboat on an ocean.

"Hi Steve," I remember now that he only stayed a day in Elizabeth Harbour before moving on. "That looks beautiful."

"Thanks. Did you sail alone to get here?"

"No, I have crew," I reply. "And you?"

"Solo."

"How was it?"

"Great, no problems."

"I didn't have the nerve to do it alone."

"I have to finish painting before it all dries,"

he says. "And unfortunately I'm meeting some friends tonight. How long are you staying?" he turns back to his work.

"I think we have to leave tomorrow. My crew doesn't have much time for this."

"Are you heading for the Med?," he asks.

"Yes."

"I've got to go to the UK. But perhaps we'll meet up again sometime."

"I hope so."

I don't dare ask him for his email address or even some leftover paint. He seems happy and at peace with himself and not at all lonely. I wish I was with him instead of James. That's the trouble with being with someone – most people imagine that James and I are a couple. How can I tell Steve that I am single and available and would love to get to know him? He concentrates on his painting and I walk slowly away admiring the other murals. My life would be so much better with the right man. They say that the most important decision one makes in life is choosing one's partner. I guess I've been making the wrong choices all my life. Perhaps I should spend some time alone, like Steve and not latch on to the next man who comes along.

I feel lonelier among people than I do in the

middle of the ocean. I imagine that they have busy, happy lives, full of friends and family. They laugh and chatter. Children and teens mingle among adults and I miss my sons. Finally, I find James in a bar but he is talking to the bartender and ignores me, so I leave. I go back to Eidos and cry myself to sleep.

17. The final stretch

Tuesday, July 27.

We leave Horta for Ponta Delgada on Ilha de São Miguel, the next island in the Azores chain, 150 nautical miles away or two days of sailing. I start the engine and James drops the dock lines. The barometer predicts good weather and the sea is calm, the sky mostly clear, no wind. A creamy orange sun rises shimmering through the waves as we motor out of the harbour with just the main up to steady the boat. After a couple of hours, James shuts the engine off, I unfurl the jib and we are able to slowly sail.

All is well but a few miles to the north, between Terceira Island and Sao Miguel, is a large, undersea volcano called Dom Joao de Castro Bank, only 43 feet under the surface. I hope it doesn't blow just now. Between December 1998 and March 2000, there were several submarine eruptions just west of Terceira with floating volcanic lava balloons steaming on the surface. Yikes!

Both of us are now eager to finish this voyage.

Wednesday, July 28.

Sao Miguel Island is the main tourist island of the Azores due to its size and the natural attraction of two lakes in old craters, Lagoa Verde and Lagoa Lazul. The sun is low on the horizon of the second day when we finally see the hills of the island in the distance. We arrive at sunset and slip into the harbour.

The next morning, we hitchhike to Furnas, in the middle of the island, to see the hot springs and geysers. The village is near three active volcanoes and the geysers are there to remind everyone of how risky this place is to live in and visit. The western caldera is partially filled by a crater lake, Lagoa das Furnas and has several fumaroles and mud pools. Centres of hydrotherapy that were built in the 19th century are also nearby. The locals are more relaxed about living here and cook food by wrapping it in leaves and placing it in the earth near the thermals. It is supposedly a treat to eat cooked this way, but it doesn't appeal to us because the food absorbs the smell of the geysers which we find a bit revolting. After an hour, we gladly descend back to the harbour.

I have no money left, so James loans me 100 Euros to buy groceries but demands my portable GPS as security. We go shopping and top up with water. The next passage will be the final one with continental Europe as our destination.

"I'm really looking forward to our arrival in Europe," I say.

"The sooner the better as far as I'm concerned," says James.

Saturday, July 31.

We are back at sea and away from people, crowds, concrete. Our world is once again just Eidos and the ocean. A four-foot manta ray swims close behind the boat, and then some dolphins. They always make me smile.

We try to steer a bit north of our course to compensate for the south-flowing current near the coast of Portugal but it's not easy with the northeasterly wind. What I learned when I was racing is to always go more into the wind whenever you can. You can always fall off later. This point of sail is also faster than going downwind and the seas are smooth, so the ride is exciting.

I take the first watch of the night while James goes below to sleep. It's peaceful, silent, with only the ocean, the sky, and Eidos in the centre of my universe.

At sunset, a full moon rises out of the ocean. It's the second full moon this month, a rare blue moon, and a third full moon of this voyage. I feel at peace. A calm sense of being at one with the universe embraces me. Perhaps being alone is not all that bad after all.

Portugal is 800 miles away – the same distance as our first passage from the Bahamas to Bermuda but so different. We are now experienced ocean voyagers, and it feels like a day sail by comparison. That first passage also began on the full moon. We've been at this for two months and I now feel confident and assured.

At midnight, a container ship passes us a mile away. I call them on the radio and get a weather report. We are to have light winds, just enough to get us moving and smooth seas. There is a cyclonic system to our north, but too far away to cause us worry.

Sunday, August 1

In the morning, a single giant, black cloud looking like a wall, threatens on the eastern horizon. We are heading straight for it.

"Come and look at this," I call out to James who is down below resting.

"So, what do you want to do about it?", he says.

"I sure hope it's not heading our way. That looks awful."

The wind is blowing from the north at 12 knots but there is no way we can go around this monster. It looks like it'll run us down. This area is well known for gale-force winds. Was the weather report wrong?

But by the afternoon, the cloud dissolves and disappears as if it was never there. The sky is now mostly clear. Where did it go? Is it hiding to pounce on us unexpectedly? The wind keeps shifting and we're getting impatient to get to Portugal, so we're tweaking the sails as much as possible. Perhaps life is like that too many of the things we worry about or fear are just figments of our imagination and if not, quite often they dissolve all by themselves without any action from us. All we need to do is adjust to the forces outside of our control, like the wind.

We have 532 nautical miles to go but now it's just a number. It's like when I used to work in a bank and had to count the money in my till at the end of the day. After a while the 100 dollar bills just became pieces of paper, I couldn't attach any value to them. And so now, miles on the GPS are just numbers, they mean nothing, 500 doesn't have any more value than 5,000 or 50, it's all an ocean. It's what's here that's important. Today, the important things are the clouds, the birds, the dolphins, and the ships that pass by. But I still mark our position on the chart every day and enjoy seeing the line joining the marks get longer and longer and closer to our destination even at half an inch at a time.

Monday, August 2.

A Norwegian ship passes us. The weather report we receive from the officer on watch is for light north-west winds for the next 48 hours. No gale warnings. They could see us from seven miles away on their radar and the seas are flat. They're moving at 14 knots. If they're watching the radar, they can avoid us, but if not, they could hit us in half an hour. We can only see them from about two miles because Eidos is so much lower from the surface of the sea.

"Ask him about his ship," says James.

"How many on board?" I ask.

"22."

"Do you see any other ships on your radar?" I repeat James' whispered questions.

"Yes. There is a sailing vessel to my north about 10 miles behind. And a ship 20 miles to the east.

"A sailboat!" I am now excited. Perhaps we'll get to see it.

"How big is your ship?"

"300 meters long, 50 m wide."

"How big is the engine?"

"15,000 horsepower"

"Ours is 20. What's your cargo?"

"1 million barrels of oil – 140 tons."

"What about the crew? Where are they from?"

"Poland."

"Dzien dobry panu." I surprise him with my Polish greeting and for the next half an hour he becomes my brother in the middle of the ocean.

Small world.

James and I travelled to Poland a couple of years ago when we were still a couple. I feel a bit of nostalgia for my home town, and for the village near Warsaw where my grandfather lived, and of course, the Baltic where with my mother, grandmother and sister, I spent many summers. But Poland is no longer my home. I need the sun and the sea. Poland is too cold in winter and the sun is just as pale as the one in Canada. I long for Greece.

18. Crossing shipping lanes

Thursday, August 5.

Clouds are forming around us and the colour of the ocean has turned from deep inky blue to grey with white foam where Eidos passes. There have been no ships since last night – the ocean is empty. We are close-hauled to a northeasterly wind and doing a comfortable 4.5 knots, a running pace. The wind vane is moaning and squeaking again while the steering cable is grinding on the steering quadrant under the cockpit floor as if it had teeth. I hope it keeps working until I get to my winter harbour. The binnacle stays put, lashed down to the cockpit spinnaker winches and stern cleats for added safety.

"I hope nothing else breaks before we get

there," says James.

"Me too." I have grown sensitive to the sounds that Eidos makes, like a mother with a newborn.

Later, from another ship, we get an update on the weather. There is a deep low off the coast of Newfoundland with 999 millibars of pressure in the centre heading northeast. It now has a name – Alex, a category 3 hurricane, with winds up to 120 knots. It formed off the coast of the U.S. on July 31, one day after we left the Azores. At one point it was only 360 miles from Bermuda. It is far enough away not to worry us but I'm glad we left the Bahamas when we did. There is a narrow window of time for this crossing. Until May, the North Atlantic still threatens with its winter storms, and after June, the hurricanes begin to spawn. The Atlantic is not a benign ocean and doesn't care for one small yacht in the middle of it.

"Hey, look at that!" James is pointing ahead.

"A sailboat!" I stare at it with incredulity as it appears out of the mist. It's the first one we have seen out on the open sea since we started this voyage. I call them on the radio. They are heading to the Azores on a delivery. I tell them about the hurricane and wish them luck. I hope they are not going any further than the Azores or they might run into bad weather.

In the afternoon, we see a ship one mile away heading south.

"I wonder where it's going, there is nothing south of here," I say. "Only more ocean". Until now, the ships have been travelling east and west.

"This must be the edge of the shipping route heading to and from the Med," says James.

"Already?"

"Yup, we're getting close. Better keep a good watch from now on."

The visibility is good so we can see them and we assume that they can see us.

That night, we learn to identify and distinguish between ships of different sizes, as well as ones with tows, by their lights. We have entered one of the busiest shipping lanes in the world.

Thursday, August 6.

Hurricane Alex is 1300 miles north of us, so not likely to affect us, but still on the same ocean as we are. Considering the hurricane season began on June first, so far we've had a lucky escape. If I hadn't found a crew, I would probably still be near. I could have easily lost my boat if not to Alex, then to one of the other hurricanes that are likely to pummel the Caribbean and the eastern U.S. in the next few months. Meanwhile, today we are sailing under blue skies, with fair winds pulling our sails like wings of a seagull.

We cross two sea mounts – large underwater mountains, that come to within 100 feet of the surface – all the way from 15,000-foot depth. In bad weather, this could be a dangerous place. Waves could pile up here in an upwelling. There seems to be a danger of some sort lurking everywhere we sail with no way of avoiding it.

The sun doesn't stay around for long. Soon, clouds gather all around us creating a heavy overcast sky and I shiver with the cold. The ocean once again turns from deep inky blue to submarine grey. Visibility decreases.

Friday, August 7

We manage to cover 107 miles in the last 24 hours – a record for us. Eidos can sail faster, but we've been sailing conservatively to stay safe. But now, as we get closer to our destination, we are getting brave and setting more sail. The clouds have disappeared and once again we are sailing on a smooth sea under a clear sky. James is no longer worried about the mast coming down and we are sailing under full main and jib.

"I'm starting to get attached to this old lady," says James. "She is a good boat."

"Not bad at all, she got us across." I smile at James and he returns a half a smile.

By the evening we have 126 miles left to go before reaching Portugal. I pull the cruising guide off the shelf and check the arrival information. James reads the Lonely Planet travel guide and plans his trip home.

Saturday, August 8.

By the end of the day, we manage to sail another 90 miles with 70 left to go to Cabo de São Vicente, our nearest landmark. The wind is light so the engine is on. We see more ships on the horizon.

At night they look like rising stars in the east, but I know each one is a danger and announce our position over the VHF radio. We also pay more attention to the colour of their lights. If we see red, it means the ship is moving from right to left. Green means it is moving from left to right and a white light means it is heading away from us. Both red and green at the same time close together mean that Eidos and the ship are on a collision course and we had better do something. Luckily, this doesn't happen often and when it does, we alter course by 10 degrees to starboard to get out of the way. Even though sailing vessels have a right of way over engine powered ones, we don't assume that they can see us or manoeuvre quickly enough to avoid a collision. They could easily run us over and not even notice.

There are container ships, tankers, tugs pulling tows, fishing boats, and God knows what else, heading for or away from Gibraltar, north and south America, northern Europe, and Africa. We have to cross this lane. It feels like driving on a multi-way, multi-lane roundabout full of semi-trailer trucks with Eidos in the middle, like an elderly person with a cane trying to cross. None of the ships can stop or alter their course for us. We have to dodge them by speeding up or slowing down as the ships push on relentlessly toward their destination. One more day of this and we should be safe.

19. Portugal

Sunday, August 9.

The next morning as we approach the westernmost coast of the European continent, all we see in front of us is a massive white fog bank that obscures our view of land and all those ships speeding all around us. Eidos has no radar, only a small aluminium reflector near the top of the mast, which hopefully places a small dot on their radar screen.

"Sécurité, Sécurité, Sécurité, this is sailing yacht Eidos." I tremble as I speak into the microphone, giving our position and heading. No one answers but I hope they are listening.

All morning, Cabo de São Vicente refuses to show its steep, high forehead out of the fog. There are two lighthouses there, somewhere. One, built over the ruins of a 16th-century convent with a light that has a range of nearly 32 miles stands to the northeast. It is one of the most powerful lights in Europe, guarding one of the world's busiest shipping lanes. But we don't see it through the fog.

"Hey, listen, B," says James. "I hear something."

I try to isolate the sounds that are all around me, the engine, the waves splattering against the hull, the wind.

Then I hear it. A low, booming moan of the foghorn. It is too faint to determine where it's coming from, but given where we are, it must be the Cabo de São Vicente one. I count the seconds: two long blasts and then silence. Two more and silence. I check my cruising guide.

"That's it. Cape St. Vincent," I say.

"But that's not where we're going," says James.

"No, but it's good to hear it."

We have to steer further south, toward a second lighthouse, at Ponta de Sagres. This one has a range of only 12 miles and we can't see it either. I read our position from the GPS and plot it on a new chart, one of the Portuguese coast. According to my mark on it, we are getting near and I steer closer to the invisible shore and safely out of the shipping lanes.

It is only a relative safety. The perpendicular cliffs rise out of the sea 250 feet up but we can only see the part of them where they touch the sea about 300 feet away. Swell and waves hurl at the rocks and I wonder what it would be like here during a storm.

No wonder this part of Europe has been called the end of the world. It fits perfectly with the picture of ships falling off a cliff in a cascading waterfall. I can imagine what Columbus must have felt heading west to the unknown, while most people still believed that the world was flat and only dragons lived beyond the horizon. I am also in a similar place, in thick fog with only the unknown blank slate of my future. Although my voyage has been in the opposite direction to Columbus, I hope that here I will also discover a new world and a new life.

I check the depth sounder display and steer Eidos following the 30-foot contour line to avoid any underwater rocks close to shore, yet safely out of the shipping channel. A fishing boat appears out of the fog ahead of us and I change course to avoid it. We watch out for small yellow floats that mark the location of the fishing nets. The nets themselves are deep below but we don't want to catch the floats and their mooring lines.

"What the... Watch out!" says James.

I follow his outstretched arm with my eyes.

About 100 feet away behind and to our port, a fast-moving sailboat, motoring, sails down, is heading in our direction. There is no one in the cockpit. I turn the wheel to starboard. As the boat overtakes us, I pull out my CO2 horn and press the button on top which jolts us with its piercing screech. A man pokes his head out of the cabin, so I put my hand over my ear, indicating the radio. He replies to my call.

"Have you seen us?" I ask.

"No, I was below."

"Do you have a radar?"

"Yes, that's why I was below." He sounds nonchalant.

"But you didn't see us. Are you not worried about colliding with something?" I'm getting frustrated.

"I have a radar. I can see everything."

"But you didn't see us. Why are you motoring so fast?"

"I'm in a hurry to get to Gibraltar."

"Good luck."

"Idiot," says James.

I hope he does manage to get to Gibraltar

safely but I don't think he is acting safely.

We could see him without radar and because we are going slowly, we could manoeuvre around in time to avoid a collision. He, on the other hand, is taking a big risk of hitting something. Many fishing boats don't even have radar reflectors.

We pass Ponta de Sagres somewhere above us and the fog slowly lifts, revealing more fishing boats in the distance and clay cliffs surrounding a bay with a sandy beach at its head. Soon, the sun succeeds in burning off the rest of the mist. People inch like ants up and down the cliff trail to the beach, carrying sun umbrellas, baskets, and blankets. Open umbrellas dot the beach like colourful mushrooms.

"This looks like a nice place to stop," I say to James.

"Good idea."

I motor in a circle around the bay while watching the depth sounder to make sure there are no underwater rocks within our swinging circle and drop the anchor in 15 feet of water. There is a slight swell, but we're tired and this is the first place with a sandy bottom and a possible landing place for the dinghy. I reverse the engine to set the anchor and then shut it off. With the engine silent, the noise from land becomes more apparent. We hear cars, people, fishing boats, music from a ghetto blaster on the beach. Civilization.

"We've done it, B," says James. He sounds relieved.

"Yes, we made it." I am astonished that we have finally arrived in Europe. Although the Azores belong to Europe as well, continental Europe feels more like home.

"I feel a bit sad that it's over," I say.

"Weren't you scared? Of drowning? With all that water?" says James.

"I couldn't let myself think about it. If I had, I'd probably curl up in a corner and whimper."

A friend who taught me to rock climb, said to just focus on the next hand or foothold and don't look up or down. This way of thinking also seemed to work at sea.

While James sorts his backpack, I make a note in the logbook. August 9, weather, wind, our position and this – 40 days and 40 nights since leaving the Bahamas.

With all the ship traffic nearby and the open sea just a few miles away, the anchorage is exposed to swell. Eidos is rolling sideways to the waves. There is surf on the beach so landing the dinghy is not a good idea. I check the cruising guide again and learn that this coast has big tides and water that is 12 feet deep at high tide can easily be 2 feet at low water. We stay on board and rest. Baleeira fishing harbour is a few miles to the east. We'll go there tomorrow.

Monday, August 10

The next morning James hauls up the anchor and we motor to the fishing harbour. We moor to the village quay next to some fishing boats and walk to a small town perched on the cliffs. This is the middle of the tourist season and people crowd the sidewalks, shops, and restaurants. The shops display beach mats, garish t-shirts and postcards outside their doors. There is a long queue at the bank machine. Scooters and cars zip up and down the streets. There are beaches for swimming on the south coast and for windsurfing to the west. Cabo de São Vicente Vicente lighthouse and the fort where Henry the Navigator established his school of navigation in preparation for the exploration of the unknown world are main tourist attractions. I feel overwhelmed by the bustle of civilization after the silence of the ocean and want to go back to Eidos as soon as possible.

We check in with the harbour authority and immigration and then find an Internet cafe where I check my email. I have a message from a sailing magazine editor – one of my articles has been accepted and I will get $300 for it. I am ecstatic. I also read in the news that Hurricane Alex wreaked havoc on the east coast of the U.S., near where we were sailing only two months ago on our way to Bermuda.

Before returning to the boat, James finds the bus station and schedule for his return to England.

Back on Eidos, James packs his backpack, takes it out on deck and heaves it onto his back. He smiles briefly, shakes my hand goodbye.

"That was a good trip. Call me if you need crew again," he says.

Over my dead body, comes to mind but I say nothing and smile because he has my spare GPS as security for the money he loaned me in the Azores and I want it back as soon as possible. I watch his back as he climbs the trail leading to the town to make sure he leaves.

From now on, I promise myself to love only those who love me and who treat me with respect. Love at any price is not worth the cost.

20. Another beginning

Don't make someone a priority in your life when you're only an option in theirs.

Solitary trees if they grow at all, grow strong.
Winston Churchill

August 11.

Eidos and I are now back to our essential selves. I am free, alone and can do whatever I want. Stay where I am, leave, sleep as long as I like, get up in the middle of the night. Eat what I like. Cook or not cook. I have a new life. My only long term plan is to find a safe harbour for the winter.

The wind and the waves caress Eidos' hull. On deck, most of the varnish I so carefully applied in the Bahamas has peeled off, stripped by the ocean and the sun. I have no money to buy more. At first, I feel sad over the loss, because it took a lot of work to put it on, but then decide to let the teak weather. Come to think of it, I haven't worn make up for the past ten weeks either and my hair is a mess. We'll both go for the natural look.

The sky is clear, so I untie the dock lines and motor back to Ponta de Sagres for some photos. Eagles, falcons, and kites soar above the cliffs. I can now see both lighthouses. No, it would not be easy to leave this shore and head into the unknown as the captains and crew did long ago. I turn Eidos around and head east.

The swell eases as Eidos moves away from the open ocean but the fog returns. I slow down and once again follow the 10-meter contour. The charts are in meters now and it's a bit scary to see 10 on the display instead of 30 but I soon get used to it.

As the fog clears in the late morning, I scan the coast lightly dotted with houses and note small coves and beaches where I could drop my hook. Could this be my new home? Or perhaps the next bay around the corner? I put the Mozart Concerto in the slot of the CD player and turn the volume up. A hawk sails above the cliffs. The sea is calm, the wind light and the sky is blue. I am in the right place, at the right time with the right person.

May your boat be leak-free. May your sails be in good repair.
May the winds be fair, the weather kind and may your days be filled with the exquisite pleasure of new adventures, fabulous destinations and excellent friendships.

~~~_/)
~~~

Acknowledgements

There are many people who helped bring this book to completion. But first, I would like to thank those who encouraged me in my early efforts, when as a newly hatched freelancer, I sent my manuscripts to sailing magazines such as 48°North, Sail, Latitudes & Attitudes, Boat Works, Living Aboard, and later Yachting Monthly and Practical Boat Owner.

I received much encouragement from Richard Hazelton, editor at 48°North magazine, now retired, who published my early efforts and even remembered who I was when I arrived unannounced in his office one day.

Thank you to Peter Nielsen, editor at Sail magazine, who at one point wrote that he liked my musings and welcomed more of them. I much appreciated your kind words, Peter and they kept me going for months.

Alison Wood, features editor at Practical Boat Owner has treated me like a friend right from the beginning of our association and dug out one of my submissions from the nearly forgotten file after a change of staff.

Theo Stocker, the editor at Yachting Monthly has also been kind and surprised me with a winner of the month prize for one of my stories.

This book had its start as a 1,500 word entry to a contest for the best anchoring story, that I submitted to 48°North. I won second prize, a winch handle for it. Later, I included it in my first book, Salt Water In My Veins. The story grew from that article into the book that you are holding now.

It has taken several years of writing and putting it away, letting it simmer, and then letting others read and critique it. I would like to thank my critique group on Scribophile, who made encouraging comments and helped me avoid glaring errors.

Much appreciation goes to my beta readers: Nancy and Richard Sequest, Pauline Scrimgeour, Gareth Hodkinson, Asunción Belliure, and Justin Smith (who also happens to be my son). You have helped in the final push to get this baby out into the world.

And finally, thank you, James of Yorkshire, wherever you may be for helping during the Atlantic crossing. Without your assistance, the voyage (and the book) might have never happened. I still have a soft spot in my heart for you.

Barbara Molin, Vonitsa, Greece, June 2020.

~~~_/)
~~~

Manufactured by Amazon.ca
Bolton, ON